Gingrich vs. Paul On The Issues

**Jesse Gordon,
OnTheIssues.org**

Table of Contents

Paul vs. Gingrich on International Issues 105

Book reviews 139

Paul vs. Gingrich on VoteMatch 152

Paul vs. Gingrich On The Issues

Representative Ron Paul of Texas and Former Speaker of the House Newt Gingrich of Georgia currently stand as two of the top-tier frontrunners for the 2012 Republican presidential nomination. This book outlines their stances on the issues, in a side-by-side manner for each issue, on many of controversial topics that they will face as President.

We gather the two candidates' issue stances from their political autobiographies; from debates in both the 2011 election season and past elections; from public speeches; from campaign websites; and from political analysis websites. All of the excerpts appear, with many additional issue stances, on our website, www.OnTheIssues.org.

Gingrich is most famous for organizing the "Contract With America" which resulted in the Republican takeover of the House of Representatives in 1994 (not to be confused with the 2010 "Contract From America"). Paul is most famous for inspiring the online revolution which initiated the Tea Party movement. This book explores the issues underlying both of those revolutions.

The purpose of this book, and the mission of our website, is to inform voters about candidates' issue stances—what they believe about the issues, and what they have done to implement those beliefs. The mainstream media report on candidates' politics: who's ahead this week; who "won" the last debate; who has endorsed whom. We reject the "horse race politics" that dominates the mainstream media, and instead focus on what matters: Paul on the issues versus Gingrich on the issues.

—Jesse Gordon, Editor-in-Chief, jesse@OnTheIssues.org
December 2011

Dedication

To Julien

Acknowledgments

This book would not have been possible without the tireless efforts of the entire OnTheIssues team: Derek Camara, Janice Gordon, Michele Gordon, Peter Hoerr, Ram Lau, Adam Leighton, Jamie Leighton, Naomi Lichtenberg, Ogden Porter, Will Rico, Dan Teittinen, Irma Teittinen, and especially Kathleen Camara.

Paul vs. Gingrich
on Domestic Issues

Domestic issues focus on joint state-federal jurisdiction or enforcement, including the following topics:

•*Crime:* including mandatory sentencing and the death penalty. Rep. Paul opposes both on libertarian grounds; Rep. Gingrich demonstrates on these issues that he is no libertarian.

•*Gun Control:* Both candidates agree on an individual right rather than a collective right to gun ownership.

•*Drugs:* including marijuana legalization and the War on Drugs. This issue differentiates Paul's libertarian hands-off approach versus Gingrich's approach of increased enforcement.

•*Environment:* including pollution and EPA issues. Gingrich demonstrates the classical conservationist attitude, and hence is more the environmentalist than Paul's property rights-based approach.

•*Technology and Infrastructure:* including high-tech Internet and privacy issues, as well as low-tech roads and bridges investment issues. Gingrich is a futurist on this issue (as he is on many issues); Paul focuses on the dangers of "Big Brother" government (as he does on many issues).

•*Health Care:* including federal healthcare and ObamaCare issues; plus Medicare/Medicaid and state issues. The two candidates try to outdo each other in opposing ObamaCare (which has become a recurring theme at the GOP primary debates), both offering state-based and market-based solutions.

Ron Paul
on Domestic Issues

Newt Gingrich
on Domestic Issues

Paul on Mandatory Sentencing

Voted YES on funding for alternative sentencing instead of more prisons

Vote on an amendment that would reduce the funding for violent offender imprisonment by and truth-in-sentencing programs by $61 million. The measure would increase funding for Boys and Girls Clubs and drug courts by the same amount.

Source: Amendment sponsored by Scott, D-VA; Bill HR 4690;
vote number 317 on June 22, 2000

Voted NO on more prosecution and sentencing for juvenile crime

Vote to pass a bill to appropriate $1.5 billion to all of the states that want to improve their juvenile justice operations. Among other provisions this bill includes funding for development, implementation, and administration of graduated sanctions for juvenile offenders, funds for building, expanding, or renovating juvenile corrections facilities, hiring juvenile judges, probation officers, and additional prosecutors for juvenile cases.

Source: Bill introduced by McCollum, R-FL; Bill HR 1501;
vote number 233 on June 17, 1999

Gingrich on Mandatory Sentencing

3-strike laws are constitutional; enforce courts compliance

Anyone who thinks the various decisions of the Supreme Court are not adequately worrisome need only look at the Ninth Circuit Court of Appeals to see how far the Left-liberals will go and how domination by secular Left-liberal judges will change America.

For example, consider the following Ninth Court decisions:

- *Andrade v. Attorney General of California*, (2001): The Ninth Circuit said the California three-strikes law was unconstitutional; the Supreme Court reversed it.

- *Summerlin v. Stewart*, (2003): The Ninth Circuit ruled that death sentences must be enacted by a jury, and not a judge, and that the ruling applied retroactively, voiding the death sentences of over 100 inmates. The Supreme Court reversed the retroactive ruling.

When a court is reversed this often, it clearly fails to meet the "good behavior" test of the Constitution. The good behavior test should be enforced. It would certainly focus the Ninth Circuit's attention on survival rather than radicalism.

Source: Winning the Future, by Newt Gingrich, p. 58-60, Oct. 1, 2005

NOTE: "Three Strikes" laws mandate that criminal offenders are sentenced to life imprisonment upon their third criminal conviction. The term refers to the baseball rule, "Three Strikes and You're Out."

Paul on Death Penalty

Too many capital convictions
have been proven errors

There was a time I simply stated that I supported the death penalty. Now my views are not so clearly defined. I do not support the federal death penalty, but constitutionally I cannot, as a federal official, interfere with the individual states that impose it. After years spent in Washington, I have become more aware than ever of the government's ineptness and the likelihood of its making mistakes.

I no longer trust the U.S. government to invoke and carry out a death sentence under any condition. Too many convictions, not necessarily federal, have been found to be in error, but only after years of incarcerating innocent people who later were released on DNA evidence. Rich people when guilty are rarely found guilty and sentenced to death. For me it's much easier just to eliminate the ultimate penalty and incarcerate the guilty for life—in case later evidence proves a mistaken conviction.

Source: Liberty Defined, by Rep. Ron Paul, p. 32-33, April 19, 2011

Gingrich on Death Penalty

Voted NO on replacing death penalty with life imprisonment

Amendment to replace death penalty crimes in the 1994 Omnibus Crime Bill with life imprisonment.

Source: Bill HR 4092; vote number 107 on April 14, 1994

More prisons, more enforcement, effective death penalty

Gingrich wrote the Contract with America:

[As part of the Contract with America, within 100 days we pledge to bring to the House Floor the following bill]:

The Taking Back Our Streets Act:

An anti-crime package including stronger truth in sentencing, "good faith" exclusionary rule exemptions, effective death penalty provisions, and cuts in social spending from this summer's crime bill to fund prison construction and additional law enforcement to keep people secure in their neighborhoods and kids safe in their schools.

Source: Contract with America on Sept. 27, 1994

Paul on Gun Rights

Opposes the DC Gun Ban;
it's not just a "collective right"

An appeals court in Washington DC issued a ruling that hopefully will result in the restoration of 2nd Amendment rights in the nation's capital. It appears the Court rejected the nonsensical argument that the 2nd Amendment confers only a "collective right," something gun control advocates have asserted for years. Rights, by definition, are individual. "Group rights" is an oxymoron.

When the 2nd Amendment speaks of a "well-regulated militia," it means local groups of individuals operating to protect their own families, homes, and communities. They regulated themselves because it was necessary and in their own interest to do so. The Founders themselves wrote in the Federalist papers about the need for individuals to be armed.

Gun control makes people demonstrably less safe—as any honest examination of criminal statistics reveals. It is no coincidence that violent crime flourishes in the nation's capital, where the individual's right to self-defense has been most severely curtailed.

Source: Weekly column, "Texas Straight Talk," March 12, 2007

Gingrich on Gun Rights

Don't redefine Constitution
with no individual right to arms

Over the last 50 years the Supreme Court has become a permanent constitutional convention in which the whims of five appointed lawyers have rewritten the meaning of the Constitution. Under this new, all-powerful model of the Court—and by extension the trail-breaking 9th Circuit Court—the Constitution and the law can be redefined, unchecked, by federal judges.

Anyone who thinks various Supreme Court decisions are not adequately worrisome need only look at the 9th Circuit Court of Appeals to see how domination by secular Left-liberal judges will change America. It is hard to imagine that one court could be so out of step with the views of the vast majority of the American people. And it is unforgivable that this destructive pattern could have been going on for a generation without an effective challenge.

For example, consider the following 9th Court decision: *Silveira v. Lockyear*, (2002): The 9th Circuit held there is no individual right to keep and bear arms.

Source: Winning the Future, by Newt Gingrich, p. 57-59, Oct. 1, 2005

NOTES: The "9th Circuit Court" refers to a federal court which is inferior to the Supreme Court. The Supreme Court later ruled on the issue of "individual rights," in the 2008 case called "District of Columbia v. Heller," that the 2nd Amendment does define an individual right to gun ownership, as opposed to a "collective right" for a state-run and state-armed National Guard.

Paul on Drugs in Society

We don't need laws to tell us to not use heroin

Q: You say that the federal government should stay out of people's personal habits, including marijuana, cocaine, even heroin.

A: It's an issue of protecting liberty across the board. If you have the inconsistency, then you're really not defending liberty. We want freedom [including] when it comes to our personal habits.

Q: Are you suggesting that heroin and prostitution are an exercise of liberty?

A: Yes, in essence, if we leave it to the states. For over 100 years, they *were* legal. You're implying if we legalize heroin tomorrow, everyone's gonna use heroin.

How many people here are going to use heroin if it were legal? I bet nobody! "Oh yeah, I need the government to take care of me. I don't want to use heroin, so I need these laws!"

I never thought heroin would get applause!

Source: 2011 GOP primary debate in South Carolina, May 5, 2011

Gingrich on Drugs in Society

Drug-free society focuses on both drug supply & demand

It is essential that we find the means to create a drug-free society for our children. As everyone knows, this has not been an easy matter for us.

The Partnership for a Drug-Free America, with its constant efforts at persuasion & education, and Nancy Reagan's "Just Say No" campaign had a real effect on drug use between 1984 and 1992. In fact, drug use declined by 2/3 in 8 years. Drug use began to rise again when the educational ad campaigns were dumped by the Clinton Administration. Now we have to launch a full-scale torrent of antidrug education, in schools, in churches, in youth organizations, in after-school programs, and everywhere else that young people hang out.

We must also raise the cost of buying and using drugs. We must find a number of economic and social penalties—not just the threat of prison which we know does not work—that will make drug use socially unacceptable. We must seal off the American border by combining [various agencies] into one focused border agency.

Source: Lessons Learned the Hard Way, by Newt Gingrich, p.204-205,
Jul 2, 1998

Paul on Marijuana Legalization

Legalize industrial hemp

Paul believes in the legalization of industrial hemp. Paul supported HR 3037 to amend the Controlled Substances Act to exclude industrial hemp from the definition of marijuana. This bill would have given the states the power to regulate farming of hemp. The measure would be a first since the national prohibition of industrial hemp farming in the United States. He favors the legalization of marijuana.

Source: SourceWatch.org, Jan. 22, 2007

NOTE: Industrial hemp is a raw material commonly used for making paper, textiles, and other commercial products. In the United States, use of industrial hemp is banned because the plant is related to marijuana. Advocates of drug legalization push the issue of industrial hemp (and wear T-shorts made of industrial hemp) because it is a marginal issue that might gain support from moderates.

Gingrich on Marijuana Legalization

Marijuana legalization would tear America apart

Gingrich now says that pot legalization would tear America apart: "Every place drugs are legalized the net effect is more people on welfare, more people who are dependent, more people with bad health care outcomes, fewer people who are able workers able to pay attention on the job and a drain of money into illegality, because immediately behind legalized marijuana comes cocaine and heroin."

Source: Tim Murphy in Mother Jones magazine, April 20, 2011

Paul on Nuclear Waste

No nuclear waste in Yucca Mountain; it's other states' garbage

Q: Do you support opening the national nuclear repository at Yucca Mountain?

PAUL: I've opposed this. I approach it from a state's rights position. What right does 49 states have to punish one state and say, "We're going to put our garbage in your state"? I think that's wrong. The government shouldn't be in the business of subsidizing any form of energy. Nuclear energy is a good source of energy, but they still get subsidies. Then we as politicians and the bureaucrats get involved with which state's going to get stuck with the garbage. The more the free market handles this and the more you deal with property rights and no subsidies to any form of energy, the easier this problem would be solved.

Source: GOP 2011 primary debate in Las Vegas, Oct. 18, 2011

NOTE: Yucca Mountain is a federally-owned mountain in Nevada which the federal government has proposed as a long-term repository for nuclear waste. Yucca Mountain was selected because, in theory, it is geologically stable enough to survive intact for the tens of thousands of years until the nuclear waste becomes harmless. The site was first proposed under President Reagan in 1985-1987; Congress approved it under President Bush in 2002; and then Congress canceled the program under President Obama in April 2011.

Gingrich on Nuclear Waste

Put nuclear waste in deep storage for 10,000 years

Q: Do you support opening the national nuclear repository at Yucca Mountain?

GINGRICH: I think that it has to be looked at scientifically. We have to find a safe method of taking care of nuclear waste. Today, because it's been caught up in a political fight, we have small units of nuclear waste all over this country in a way that is vastly more dangerous than finding a method of keeping it in a very, very deep place that would be able to sustain 10,000 or 20,000 or 30,000 years of geological safetQ: Is Yucca Mountain that place?

GINGRICH: I'm not a scientist. I mean, Yucca Mountain certainly was picked by the scientific community as one of the safest places in the US.

Q: You were for opening it in Congress, right?

GINGRICH: When I was in Congress, I worked with the Nevada delegation to make sure that there was time for scientific studies. But we have to find some method of finding a very geologically stable place, and most geologists believe that, in fact, Yucca Mountain is that.

Source: GOP 2011 primary debate in Las Vegas, Oct. 18, 2011

Paul on Animal Rights

Scored 14% on Humane Society Scorecard
on animal protection

The Humane Society 109th Congress Scorecard on animal protection scored Paul 14 out of 100, based on:

- Paul voted against the Horse Slaughter Prevention Act (HR.503): To bar slaughtering horses for human consumption.

- Paul voted for the "poison pill" Amendment delaying implementation of HR.503.

- Paul did not vote on the BLM amendment on 5/19/2005: To bar slaughtering wild horses & burros.

- Paul voted against the Pets Evacuation and Transportation Standards (PETS) Act (HR.3858): To consider the needs of people with pets and service animals in disaster planning.

- Paul did not co-sponsor the Animal Fighting Prohibition Act (S.382): To criminalize dogfighting & cockfighting.

- Paul did not co-sponsor the Downed Animal Protection Act (HR.3931): to ban "downed" (unable to walk to slaughter) cattle, pigs & sheep in human food.

- Paul did not sign the Funding Letter of 4/28/2006, to the Agriculture Appropriations Subcommittee for animal protection.

Source: Humane Society 109th Congress Scorecard, www.fund.org,
Jan 31, 2007

Gingrich on Animal Rights

Early 1980s: co-sponsored
Endangered Species Act

In the early 1980s, Gingrich took some positions that separated him from most of the right wing. He voted for the Alaska Lands Act. He cosponsored the Endangered Species Act, and the Clean Air Act. Most of his early supporters from the environmental movement long ago gave up on him, but among Republicans, he remains a bona fide conservationist. Newt argues that he has been true to his original beliefs, while the "greens" have moved in a radical direction, toward the taking of private property without adequate compensation.

Gingrich made plain in a recent interview: "We're going to try to write [an Endangered Species Act] that's economically rational and that protects species. The problem now is that the environmental movement is dominated by lawyers and bureaucrats, and it's a front for anti-free-enterprisers who use protecting species as a device to stop development. The question is, do you spend $300 million to protect one species or do you spend that money to protect 30 species?"

Source: Newt!, by Dick Williams, p.102, June 1, 1995

Paul on Environment vs. Economy

Property rights are the foundation of all rights

We must stop special interests from violating property rights and literally driving families from their homes, farms and ranches. We also face another danger in regulatory takings: Through excess regulation, governments deprive property owners of significant value and use of their properties—all without paying "just compensation."

Property rights are the foundation of all rights in a free society. Without the right to own a printing press, for example, freedom of the press becomes meaningless.

Source: 2008 House campaign website, "Issues," Sept. 1, 2007

Neglected property rights during the industrial revolution

Q: Gov. Schwarzenegger has proposed that California be allowed to implement much tougher environmental regulations on emission requirements than apply to the rest of the country. Do you side with the governor or with the Bush administration?

A: Yes, California should do what they want. When we're dealing with the environment and greenhouse gases, [it's] property rights. We neglected during the industrial revolution property rights, and governments and big corporations got together and colluded.

Source: 2008 debate at Reagan Library in Simi Valley, Jan. 30, 2008

Gingrich on Environment vs. Economy

Combine healthy environment and a healthy economy

It is possible to have a healthy environment & a healthy economy. It is possible to build incentives for a cleaner future. It is possible to have biodiversity & wealthy human beings on the same planet. And it is possible to have free markets, scientific and technological advances, and an even more positive environmental outcome. There is every reason to be optimistic that if we develop smart environmental and biodiversity policies our children & grandchildren will experience an even more pleasant world.

Source: Gingrich Communications website, www.newt.org, Dec. 1, 2006

Paul on WikiLeaks

WikiLeaks only released true but embarrassing information

Consider the case of Julian Assange, the founder of Wiki-Leaks. After he spread diplomatic documents, the long knives came out. Bill O'Reilly said that Assange was a traitor and "should be executed." Sarah Palin said that he ought to be targeted "like the Taliban." Ralph Peters of Fox News said, "I would execute leakers." Mike Huckabee said, "I think anything less than execution is too kind a penalty." Glenn Beck said Assange should be executed. G. Gordon Liddy said he should be put on a kill list.

In the end, Assange is just one man with a laptop and he was merely releasing what is true, information that embarrassed many but harmed no one. And this is the man that so many think ought to be subject to the death penalty? Government always uses it power to punish its own enemies, but its enemies are not necessarily our enemies. It's best we change our system rather than think people such as Assange, or others digging for the truth, are treasonous and should be executed.

Source: Liberty Defined, by Rep. Ron Paul, p. 35-36, April 19, 2011

NOTE: WikiLeaks is a website run by a libertarian technophile Julian Assange. In 2010, WikiLeaks got hold of millions of classified government documents that he and his organization believed should not be kept secret from the public. Many of those documents were posted on the WikiLeaks website. Assange has been under criminal investigation ever since.

Gingrich on WikiLeaks

Treat WikiLeaks as enemy combatants engaged in terrorism

Q: If you were in charge, how would you handle Julian Assange and WikiLeaks?

A: Information warfare is warfare, and Julian Assange is engaged in warfare. Information terrorism, which leads to people getting killed, is terrorism, and Julian Assange is engaged in terrorism. He should be treated as an enemy combatant. WikiLeaks should be closed down permanently and decisively. But even more, how can these documents have been released?

Q: Via a private in the Army.

A: How do you have a system so stupid [that an Army Private can] download a quarter million documents and the system doesn't say [anything]? I mean this is a system so stupid that it ought to be a scandal of the first order. This administration is so shallow, and so amateurish about national security that it is painful and dangerous.

Source: Fox News interview on Business Insider, Dec. 5, 2010

Paul on Outer Space Policy

Militarizing outer space impoverishes America

President Bush let it be known that we will assert our jurisdiction not only worldwide, but in space as well. The president declared that the US will determine which countries will have access to space. He has announced that outer space will be militarized and controlled by the US.

Wealth is transferred from the poor to the politically connected rich through the inflationary process. The pseudo-strength of the dollar allows endless money creation to pay the bills to police the world. In the US, the process manifests in the decline of living for the poor, the middle class, and the elderly.

The limits of our policies will be exposed by military failures, the loss of political support, and a rejection of the over-inflated US dollars used to pay our bills. The cost of runaway military spending essentially brought down the Soviet Union and soon will bring down N. Korea. We are doing the same thing.

Source: A Foreign Policy of Freedom, by Ron Paul, p.367, June 15, 2007

Gingrich on Outer Space Policy

Replace NASA with incentives to private sector

Q: What role should the government play in future space exploration?

GINGRICH: I'm a big fan of going into space and I worked to get the shuttle program to survive at one point. But NASA has become a case study in why bureaucracy can't innovate. If you take all the money we've spent at NASA since we landed on the moon and you had applied that money for incentives to the private sector, we would today probably have a permanent station on the moon, and a new generation of lift vehicles. And instead, what we've had is bureaucracy after bureaucracy and failure after failure. We're at the beginning of a whole new cycle of extraordinary opportunities. And, unfortunately, NASA is standing in the way of it, when NASA ought to be getting out of the way and encouraging the private sector.

PAWLENTY: I don't think we should eliminate the space program.

GINGRICH: I didn't say end the space program. I said you could get into space faster & more effectively, if you decentralized it & got it out of Washington

Source: 2011 GOP primary debate in Manchester NH, June 13, 2011

Paul on Citizen Loyalty

National ID card is part of fear-based government

As long as a government can stir up fear, sometimes real and sometimes not real, the people are expected to do one thing: sacrifice their liberty. If you're fearful, the government, the people who believe in big government—big-government conservatives or big-government liberals—they like fear to be out there.

Sometimes fear is normal & natural & real, and we have to deal with it. At other times it's concocted. In times of war, whether it was the civil war, WWI, WWII—just think of the violations of civil liberties during the period of war when people are frightened.

The one conclusion I have come to since 9/11 is that there is absolutely never a need to sacrifice any of your personal liberties to be safe! That means we do not have to accept the notion that we can have warrantless searches, a total loss of our privacy. We don't need a National ID card. You don't have to register the American people to make us safe. You have to deal with the problem much more directly.

Source: Speeches to 2008 Conservative Political Action Conference,
Feb 7, 2008

Gingrich on Citizen Loyalty

Loyalty test for everyone, not just for Muslims

Q: You've said you would impose a loyalty test for Muslims to serve in your administration. You said, "We did this in dealing with the Nazis, and we did this in dealing with the communists." What specific loyalty test would you require them to take?

GINGRICH: Actually, I didn't describe it as applied to Muslims. I described it as applied to everybody. There is nothing illegitimate about seeking to make sure that people are loyal to the US if they work for the government of the US.

I was responding to this insane moment [in a trial of] the guy who built the car bomb from Pakistan, was asked by the judge, who said to him, "But you swore an oath of loyalty to the US." And he said to the judge, "I am your enemy. I lied." The judge seemed mystified at the idea that somebody would have lied.

And my point is, we now know there really were communist spies. And I would suggest to you we need security provisions across the board to ensure that those Americans and the American government are loyal to the US.

Source: Iowa Straw Poll 2011 GOP debate in Ames Iowa, Aug. 11, 2011

Paul on Health mandate

States *can* mandate insurance, but it's a bad idea

Q: [to Romney]: Where do you find mandating authority for health insurance [as RomneyCare does] in the Constitution?

ROMNEY: Are you familiar with the Massachusetts constitution? I am. It allows states [to mandate insurance].

Q: [to Paul]: Does a state has a constitutional right to make someone buy insurance just because they're a resident?

PAUL: No, the federal government can't go in and prohibit the states from doing bad things. And I would consider that a very bad thing, but you don't send in a federal police force because they're doing it. So they do have that leeway under our Constitution. But we have drifted so far from any of our care being delivered by the marketplace. And once you get the government involved—both parties have done it—they've developed a medical care delivery system based on corporatism. The corporations are doing quite well, whether it's Obama or under the Republicans. The drug companies do well. The insurance companies do well. The patient and the doctors suffer.

Source: Iowa Straw Poll 2011 GOP debate in Ames Iowa, Aug. 11, 2011

Gingrich on Health mandate

If you mandate healthcare,
you mandate everything in life

Q: You've been very open to the individual mandate. It has become a litmus test in this Republican primary. Should it be?

A: Yes, it should be. If you explore the mandate, it ultimately ends up with unconstitutional powers. It allows the government to define virtually everything. And if you can do it for health care, you can do it for everything in your life, and, therefore, we should not have a mandate.

But I want to answer at a different level. This campaign cannot be only about the presidency. We need to pick up at least 12 seats in the Senate and 30 or 40 more seats in the House, because if you are serious about repealing Obamacare, you have to be serious about building a big enough majority in the legislative branch that you could actually in the first 90 days pass the legislation. So I just think it's very important to understand, it's not about what one person in America does. It's about what the American people do. And that requires a senatorial majority, as well as a presidency.

Source: 2011 GOP primary debate in Manchester NH, June 13, 2011

Paul on Medicare

Let people opt out of Medicare

Q: How do you propose to keep Medicare financially solvent?

PAUL: Well, under these conditions, it's not solvent and won't be solvent. If you're an average couple, you would have put $140,000 into it. And in your lifetime, you will take out more than three times that much. So a little bit of arithmetic tells you it's not solvent, so we're up against the wall on that, so it can't be made solvent. It has to change. We have to have more competition in medicine.

I would think that if we don't want to cut any of the medical benefits for children or the elderly, because we have drawn so many in and got them so dependent on the government, if you want to work a transition, you have to cut a lot of money. Some revamping has to occur. What we need is competition. We need to get a chance for the people to opt out of the system. You talk about opting out of Obamacare? Why can't we opt out of the whole system and take care of ourselves?

Source: 2011 GOP primary debate in Manchester NH, June 13, 2011

Gingrich on Medicare

Block grant Medicaid;
create individual incentives & bonuses

Q: What about Medicaid?

GINGRICH: Go to Newt.org for the proposed 21st Century Contract with America. The first step is to repeal Obamacare. [Then] block grant Medicaid. And block grant all remaining welfare programs. Give the states the power to deal with the poor using innovation and money savings.

I do not believe you solve problems under the Left's policy of people being helpless. We need to rethink Medicaid much the way we rethought welfare reform. Governor Bush in Florida had a program where people who took care of themselves and didn't go to the emergency room got a Christmas bonus. To the shock of academics, poor people were aware of money and strived to get that bonus by not abusing the emergency rooms.

If you had the ability to triage and send people to minute clinics, then the hospital wouldn't charge emergency room rates. We have to start distinguishing between the taxpayer who is concerned with charitable care and taxpayers who are suckers and are being exploited.

Source: Head-to-head debate between Herman Cain & Newt Gingrich,
Nov 5, 2011

Paul on ObamaCare

ObamaCare is only as socialized as Bush's & Nixon's reforms

Obama has been accused of pushing for socialized medicine. This is not exactly true. Maybe in time it will become a total government program. But actually his reforms are very similar to reforms pushed by the Republicans over the decades. The Republican Party under Eisenhower established the Department of Health, Education and Welfare in the 1950s. Nixon pushed through managed care ERISA laws in the early 1970s after a decade of Democrats implementing their Medicare and Medicaid programs with strong Republican support. The Reagan administration expanded medical transfer payments. Prescription drug programs were passed by the George Bush administration and a Republican Congress. And now it's the Democrats' turn once again. Republicans shout "socialized medicine" as they became the nominal opponents of Obama Care.

Source: Liberty Defined, by Rep. Ron Paul, p.196, April 19, 2011

Gingrich on ObamaCare

Repeal ObamaCare; sign tort reform instead

President Obama could be bipartisan. There are seven steps to the center for Obama.

1. Sign the repeal of ObamaCare. 58% of the American people, in the most recent poll, favor repeal of ObamaCare.

2. Sign Tort reform for doctors. He said the other night he would like to do it, let's let him do it.

3. Sign the permanent repeal of the death tax.

4. Sign a new Hyde Amendment, so no tax payer money funds abortion in the United States.

5. Sign a new Conservative Budget Act, to control spending and move to a balanced budget.

6. Sign a law to decisively control the border now.

7. Sign a tenth amendment implementation act returning power from Washington to the states and to the people thereof. And that act should include—to prove how real it is—block-granting Medicaid so that states can control the cost and improve the quality without interference from Washington bureaucrats.

Now, I hope you'd agree with me that a President Obama that did those seven things would have come to the center.

Source: Speech at 2011 Conservative Political Action Conference,
Feb 11, 2011

Paul vs. Gingrich
on Economic Issues

Economic issues focus on the recession recovery and all fiscal matters, including the following topics:

- *Budget & Economy:* including deficit spending and all aspects of the federal budget. Rep. Paul's ideas about ending the Federal Reserve, once considered extremist, have become mainstream. Gingrich focuses on the mainstream GOP supply-side solutions. Paul's ideas on returning to the gold standard are still considered extremist.

- *Corporations:* including corporate taxation and corporate welfare. Paul focuses on the dangers of concentrated power, while Gingrich focuses on minimizing corporate regulation.

- *Government Reform:* focusing on the size of the federal government, which Paul and Gingrich agree should be smaller and more restricted.

- *Jobs:* including unemployment and union issues, but not the underlying economic sources of job growth and loss (that's covered in the economic issues section). The two candidates agree on restricting unions and limiting unemployment compensation.

- *Social Security:* including the current Trust Fund and changes for the future. The two candidates agree on providing opt-out mechanisms.

- *Tax Reform:* including income taxes, tax rates, and bracket redistribution. The two candidates agree on radically reducing taxes, but Paul cites libertarian limited government, while Gingrich cites economic supply-side rationales.

Ron Paul
on Economic Issues

Newt Gingrich
on Economic Issues

Paul on Financial Bailout

Don't bail out banks; bail out homeowners

Q: [to Cain]: Regarding "Occupy Wall St.," you said, "Don't blame Wall Street, don't blame the big banks. If you don't have a job, and you're not rich, blame yourself." Do you still say that?

CAIN: Yes, I do still say that. They might be frustrated with Wall Street and the bankers, but they're directing their anger at the wrong place. They ought to be over in front of the White House taking out their frustration.

PAUL: I think Mr. Cain has blamed the victims. There's a lot of people that are victims of this business cycle. We can't blame the victims. I'd go to Washington as well as Wall Street, but I'd go over to the Federal Reserve. The bailouts came from both parties. The banks were involved, and the Federal Reserve was involved. But who got stuck? The middle class got stuck. They got stuck. They lost their jobs, and they lost their houses. If you had to give money out, you should have given it to people who were losing their mortgages, not to the banks.

Source: GOP 2011 primary debate in Las Vegas, Oct. 18, 2011

Gingrich on Financial Bailout

Insure banks rather than pass out checks

The Path to Socialist Banking:

1. In Sep. 2008, the major brokerage houses teeter on the brink of bankruptcy.

2. President Bush and his Treasury secretary propose a huge bailout to inject $700 billion of capital into falling financial institutions to stabilize them and stop a run on their assets. The plan is called Troubled Assets Relief Program (TARP).

3. Republicans in the House try to stop the bill (they had the majority then) and substitute an approach masterminded by former House speaker Newt Gingrich to insure banks rather than pass out checks to them. The House defeats the Bush bailout proposal.

4. John McCain "suspends" his campaign; the Republicans in the House cave in at the behest of their nominee and agree to TARP.

5. Democrats ask, what will the taxpayer get out of the TARP bailouts? Had the Republicans listened to Gingrich, the question would have had no force, since no money would have changed hands. But in the context of the Bush TARP bill, the question demands an answer.

Source: Take Back America, by Dick Morris, p.103-105, April 13, 2010

Paul on Automaker Bailout

Auto company nationalization is fascism

The failure of the economy and the loss of the moral foundation have now set the stage for nationalization. Do the auto executives come to Washington to demand freedom? Do they demand a sound currency that would rectify the international trade imbalances?

No, they come to Washington to demand that innocent Americans bail them out & protect a system that deserves no protection. They beg to be taken over, nationalized, to obey a car czar and sacrifice every bit of self-respect that they might retain.

There's a lot of blame to go around for bringing us to this point: the Fed, the Congress, the courts. But the most abhorrent is the failure of the giants of industry to defend free markets. They are willing to be junior partners with government. Fascism is not on their mind.

I call it "nationalism without a whimper," and the corporate business community is begging for it. The nationalization of industry, while retaining private ownership in name only, is just another word for fascism.

Source: End the Fed, by Rep. Ron Paul, p.160–161, Sept. 29, 2010

Gingrich on Automaker Bailout

Bailout combines bad policy
with worst of Detroit's decay

"In an amazing display of historic ignorance, economic destructiveness, and ideologically driven dishonesty, Washington politicians are in the process of combining the worst of the 1970s bad economic policies with the worst of Detroit's economic and (America's) educational decay. We are in grave danger of turning all of America into the kind of declining economy and bureaucratic mess which Detroit became over the last forty years."—Newt Gingrich

Source: Saving Freedom, by Jim DeMint, p.124, July 4, 2009

NOTE: The federal government "bailed out" the Big Three automakers early in the 2008 Great Recession. The bailout consisted of direct loans to General Motors and Chrysler, and a line of credit for Ford Motors. President Bush approved $17 billion for GM and Chrysler beginning in 2008, with the loan contingent upon the two automakers following federal government restructuring of their companies. The purpose of the bailout was to avoid bankruptcy and a large surge in unemployment of auto workers.

Paul on Wall Street Reform

Go after crony capitalism; defend real capitalism

Q: Gov. Perry's critics in the state of Texas—you're a congressman from Texas—say he practices crony capitalism as governor. Are they right?

PAUL: I haven't analyzed it enough to call him a crony or not. But there is a lot of crony capitalism going on in this country. And that has to be distinguished from real capitalism, because this "Occupation" stuff on Wall Street, if you're going after crony capitalism, I'm all for it. Those are the people who benefit from contracts from government, benefits from all of the bailouts. They don't deserve compassion, they deserve taxation, or they deserve to have all their benefits removed. But crony capitalism isn't when somebody makes money and they produce a product. That is very important. We have to distinguish the two. And unfortunately, I think some people mix that. But this, to me, is so vital, that we recognize what capitalism is versus crony capitalism. When you have crony capitalism, and that's why we're facing this crisis today.

Source: 2011 CNBC GOP Primary debate in Rochester MI, Nov. 9, 2011

Gingrich on Wall Street Reform

Dodd-Frank kills small business & small banks

Q: [to Gingrich]; Gov. Romney has said that the government should let the foreclosure process play out so that the housing market can recover and the free markets can work. Is he right?

GINGRICH: He's certainly right that you want to get to the real value of the houses as fast as you can. But I think there are two specific steps you have got to understand in terms of housing. If the Congress would repeal Dodd/Frank, you would see the housing market start to improve overnight. Dodd/Frank kills small banks, it kills small business. The federal regulators are anti-housing loan, and it has maximized the pain level. You could also change some of the rules so it would be easier to do a short sale where the house is worth less than mortgage than it is to do a foreclosure. Today, the banks are actually profiting more by foreclosing than encouraging short sales. But in the long run, you want the housing market to come back? The economy has to come back.

Source: 2011 CNBC GOP Primary debate in Rochester MI, Nov. 9, 2011

NOTE: "Dodd/Frank" refers to Sen. Chris Dodd (D, CT) and Rep. Barney Frank (D, MA), the co-authors of the Dodd–Frank Wall Street Reform and Consumer Protection Act of 2010. The legislation was intended to reform the rules of the financial and insurance industry to avoid another "meltdown" like the one in mid-2008 which initiated the Great Recession.

Paul on Economic Stimulus

Stimulus package means more printing & devaluing the dollar

What is the bailout package all about? Our side of the aisle proposes it and the Democrats want to increase it. $150 billion? No, let's up it $200 billion! Where does it come from?—the government has no money. Well, can we tax people?—no, you can't tax anymore. What are they gonna do?—they're gonna print the money, devalue the dollar, & that's the problem we have.

The dollar is low, prices are high, the people are suffering, the middle class is shrinking. So we offer the same old pabulum, the same old baloney, and then we turn around and say, "Well, why don't we ask the Federal Reserve to create more money? Nobody seems to have enough money. If we just had more money, maybe it would prop up the stock market." So we go to the Federal Reserve and say we need more money. So they crank it out. You can't lower interest rates unless you print more money. So they lower interest rates dramatically, like never before. So we're in a bind, we're in a fix, and I'll tell you what: we overspend. Everywhere!

Source: Speeches to 2008 Conservative Political Action Conference,
Feb 7, 2008

Gingrich on Economic Stimulus

No sequel to failed stimulus & job-killing policies

Last night President Obama called for a sequel to his failed stimulus, proving he continues to support the same destructive, job-killing policies that created the Obama Depression. If the jobs weren't shovel-ready after his $800 billion stimulus, which the president himself admitted, why will this be different?

After repeatedly calling on Congress to pass his American Jobs Act immediately—we discover there is no bill and no plan to pay for it. President Obama continues to ignore facts and instead doubles down on failed economic policies. We need real leadership now that uses proven policies from the Reagan presidency and my Speakership to empower Americans to create jobs.

Source: Response to Obama's 2011 Jobs Speech, Sep 9, 2011

NOTES: The "American Jobs Act" refers to a series of legislative proposals made by President Obama beginning in Sept. 2011. Initially, the legislation was proposed as one large bill (S. 1549 and H.R. 12), but the bill stalled in Congress. Hence Obama broke up the bill into numerous smaller pieces. The key components are:

- $245 billion for Payroll tax cut extension (maintaining a reduction in the Social Security FICA deduction).

- $57 billion for extending unemployment benefits

- $65 billion for direct hiring of municipal employees, focusing on teachers, police, and firefighters

- $65 billion for infrastructure construction.

The term "shovel ready" refers to the previous round of stimulus bills, which focused on projects which could start immediately.

Paul on Reaganomics

1980s had huge deficits, despite Reagan's message

PERRY: You wrote a letter to Ronald Reagan and said I'm going to quit the party because of the things you believe in.

PAUL: I strongly supported Ronald Reagan. I was one of four members of Congress from Texas that supported Reagan in '76. And I supported him all along, and I supported all his issues and all his programs. But in the 1980s, we spent too much, we taxed too much, we built up our deficits, and it was a bad scene. Therefore, I support the message of Ronald Reagan. The message was great. But the consequence, we have to be honest with ourselves. It was not all that great. Huge deficits during the 1980s, and that is what my criticism was for, not for Ronald Reagan's message. His message is a great message.

Source: 2011 GOP debate in Simi Valley CA at the Reagan Library,
Sep 7, 2011

Gingrich on Reaganomics

Voted against Reagan tax increases
& Bush tax increases

I think we need to get independent from this leader fascination with the presidency. I voted against two Reagan tax increases. I voted against George H. W. Bush's 1990 tax increase. It is a totally honorable and legitimate thing to say I am going to support the candidate and oppose the policy. This idea [is] that I think we [did] President George W. Bush a grave disservice by not being dramatically more aggressive in criticizing when they were wrong, and being more open when they were making mistakes.

Source: Speech at 2008 Conservative Political Action Conference,
Feb 9, 2008

Paul on Federal Reserve secrecy

Fed has ominous power with no oversight & no control

In 1980, I expressed my concern to Fed Chairman Volcker that reserve requirements could be lowered to zero and the Federal Reserve could buy any asset, including foreign debt.

Volcker assured me he would never lower reserve requirements to that degree or buy up worthless assets; just the authority to have free rein in raising reserve requirements at will. I said that, although I didn't expect that he would use these extreme powers, who knew if in the future we might just have someone who would. The future is now here.

The fact is that not only has this come to pass with Bernanke, but a great deal more authority has been usurped by Fed, while Congress says little about it. The Fed today has ominous powers that Congress barely understands. There is essentially no oversight, no audit, and no control. And the Federal Reserve chairman has no obligations to answer questions. Trillions of dollars can be created and injected into the economy with no obligation by the Fed to reveal who benefits.

Source: End the Fed, by Rep. Ron Paul, p. 48–50, Sept. 29, 2010

Gingrich on Federal Reserve secrecy

The Fed's secrecy & power
are antithetical to a free society

Q: The chairman of the Federal Reserve, Ben Bernanke, will come to the end of his term in 2014. Would you reappoint Ben Bernanke?

GINGRICH: I would fire him tomorrow.

Q: Why?

GINGRICH: I think he's been the most inflationary, dangerous, and power-centered chairman of the Fed in the history of the Fed. I think the Fed should be audited. I think the amount of money that he has shifted around in secret, with no responsibility, no accountability, no transparency, is absolutely antithetical to a free society. And I think his policies have deepened the depression, lengthened the problems, increased the cost of gasoline, and been a disaster.

Source: 2011 GOP debate in Simi Valley CA at the Reagan Library,
Sep 7, 2011

Paul on Balanced Budget

Supports Balanced Budget Amendment
& on-budget accounting

Paul adopted the Republican Liberty Caucus Position Statement:

The Republican Liberty Caucus endorses the following [among its] principles:

• There should be an amendment to the US Constitution to require a balanced budget, provided it includes a supermajority requirement to raise taxes and provided it does not empower the judiciary to unilaterally raise taxes.

• Honest accounting dictates that all federal expenditures should be on budget.

• Each budget should be derived based upon the justification for and needs of each program, with no program being either budgeted for or increased automatically.

Source: Republican Liberty Caucus Position Statement, Dec. 8, 2000

Gingrich on Balanced Budget

Demand a Balanced Budget Amendment

Gingrich signed the Contract From America

The Contract from America, clause 3:

Demand a Balanced Budget:

Begin the Constitutional amendment process to require a balanced budget with a two-thirds majority needed for any tax hike.

The Contract from America, clause 6:

End Runaway Government Spending:

Impose a statutory cap limiting the annual growth in total federal spending to the sum of the inflation rate plus the percentage of population growth.

Source: The Contract From America, July 8, 2010

Paul on Term Limits

I vote for term limits, but they won't solve anything

Some argue for term limits. Though I have voted for and supported term limits, I have never held the belief that they would solve much of anything. Besides, strict term limits would require an amendment to the Constitution, and that's not going to happen.

Term limits, whether voluntary or mandated, provide no guarantee that the replacements will do a better job. In fact, it could go the other way and create incentives for new politicians to take as much as they can, hand out as much as they can, while they are able. With voluntary term limits now less popular than ever, the principled members stick to their promises and those less principled ignore their pledges to serve a certain length of time.

The only option we have under today's conditions of runaway government is to send to Washington only representatives who will have the character to resist the temptation to blend in with the crowd.

Source: Liberty Defined, by Rep. Ron Paul, p.179-180, April 19, 2011

NOTE: Currently the President is subject to an 10-year term limit (or two elective terms). Neither the House nor Senate currently have term limits; instituting them would require a Constitutional Amendment. Many governors and state legislatures do have term limits.

Gingrich on Term Limits

Limit punitive damages; term limits on Congress

Gingrich wrote the Contract with America:

[As part of the Contract with America, within 100 days we pledge to bring to the House Floor the following bills]:

The Common Sense Legal Reforms Act:

"Loser pays" laws, reasonable limits on punitive damages, and reform of product liability laws to stem the endless tide of litigation.

The Citizen Legislature Act:

A first-ever vote on term limits to replace career politicians with citizen legislators.

Source: Contract with America, Sept. 27, 1994

Paul on Earmarks

Put 65 projects into 2006 bills, worth $4B to his district

Q: You talk about opposing big government, but you seem to have a different attitude about your own congressional district. In 2006, your district received more than $4 billion: 65 earmark-targeted projects that you have put into congressional bills for your district.

A: You got it completely wrong. I've never voted for an earmark in my life.

Q: No, but you put them in the bill.

A: I put it in because I represent people who are asking for some of their money back.

Q: If you put it in the bill, and then you know it's going to pass Congress and so you don't refuse the money.

A: Well, no, of course not. It's like taking a tax credit. I'm against the taxes but I take all my tax credits. I want to get the money back for the people.

Q: If you were true to your philosophy, you would say no pork spending in my district.

A: No, no, that's not it. They steal our money, that's like saying that people shouldn't take Social Security money. I'm trying to save the system, make the system work

Source: Meet the Press: 2007 "Meet the Candidates" series,
Dec 23, 2007

Gingrich on Earmarks

Democrats say they oppose earmarks, but proposed 8,000

I listened carefully to the President's speech the other night. Obama suggests to us that he is opposed to earmarks, when the very next day the Democrats are going to bring up a bill with 8,000 earmarks in it and then to suggest that one doesn't count because they started all the pork before he got here. I was looking for change we can believe in.

And so I was startled that he was saying to us that he opposed to earmarks; [I suppose maybe] later he'll really oppose them.

Source: Speech to 2009 Conservative Political Action Conference,
Feb 27, 2009

NOTE: "Earmarks" refers to itemized spending in legislation, i.e., funding targeted toward a particular project in a particular place. The controversy comes about because often the particular place includes the home district of the legislator writing or sponsoring the bill (which is known derisively as "Pork-Barrel Spending"). Earmarks are currently legal and are generally considered ethical; earmark reform focuses on publicizing their existence and perhaps on a future Line Item Veto to remove some.

Paul on Unions

Right to organize; but no special benefits for unions

Q: Are unions good for America?

A: The right to unionize should be a basic right of any group. You should be able to organize. You should have no privileges, no special benefits legislated to benefit the unions, but you should never deny any working group to organize and negotiate for the best set of standards of working conditions.

Source: 2007 Republican debate in Dearborn, Michigan, Oct. 9, 2007

Mandated wages & unions hurt unprotected workers

Minimum wage laws & mandating union contracts (closed shop) are designed to help a small segment of workers gain economic advantage while actually hurting unprotected workers. Long term, even the beneficiaries suffer from the unemployment that excessive wage demands bring about.

Coerced union wages and dictated minimum wages grossly distort the market process and contribute to the malinvestment initiated by the Federal Reserve policy and guarantee that in the correction, wages must come down.

Source: Liberty Defined, by Rep. Ron Paul, p.309-310, April 19, 2011

Gingrich on Unions

Defund National Labor Relations Board; favor right-to-work

Q: New Hampshire could soon become the 23rd state to pass right to work legislation. Unions don't like it because it makes membership voluntary. Would you support a federal right-to-work law?

A: One of the things the Congress should do immediately is defund the National Labor Relations Board which has gone into South Carolina to punish Boeing, which wants to put 8,000 American jobs in S.C. by fundamentally eliminating right-to-work at the National Labor Relations Board. That's a real, immediate threat from the Obama administration to eliminate right to work. And I think that it is fundamentally the wrong direction.

I hope that New Hampshire does adopt right-to-work. I frankly keep it at the state level because as each new state becomes right to work, they send a signal to the remaining states, don't be stupid. If you believe in the 10th Amendment, we ought to let the states learn from each other. And the right-to-work states are creating a lot more jobs today that they heavily unionized states.

Source: 2011 GOP primary debate in Manchester NH, June 13, 2011

Paul on Unemployment Extension

Voted NO on extending unemployment benefits from 39 weeks to 59 weeks

Congressional Summary: Revises the formula for Tier-1 amounts a state credits to an applicant's emergency unemployment compensation account. Increases the figures in the formula from 50% to 80% of the total amount of regular compensation; and from 13 to 20 times the individual's average weekly benefit amount.

Proponent's argument to vote Yes:

Rep. CHARLES RANGEL (D, NY-15): Over the last 12 months the number of unemployed workers has jumped by over 2 million, leaving 10 million Americans struggling for work. These are hardworking people that have lost their jobs through no fault of their own.

Rep. JERRY WELLER (R, IL-11): This program continues the requirement that those benefiting from extended unemployment benefits had to have worked at least 20 weeks. Americans were rightly concerned about proposals to eliminate that work requirement and allow 39 weeks or, under the legislation before us today, as many as 59 weeks of total unemployment benefits to be paid to those who have previously only worked for a few weeks.

Opponent's argument to vote No:

None voiced.

Source: Unemployment Compensation Extension Act; Bill HR.6867;
vote number 683, Oct. 3, 2008

Gingrich on Unemployment Extension

Go to college instead of 99 weeks of unemployment

Q: You criticized extending unemployment benefits, saying that you were "opposed to giving people money for doing nothing." Benefits have already been extended to 99 weeks, and they are set to expire soon. If you were president today, would you extend unemployment benefits?

GINGRICH: I think unemployment compensation should be tied directly to a training program. And if you don't have a job and you need help, then in order for us to give you the help, you should sign up for a business-led training program so that that 99 weeks becomes an investment in human capital, so you can get a job. But I believe it is fundamentally wrong to give people money for 99 weeks for doing nothing. That's why we had welfare reform. The easiest thing for Congress, if the president sends up a proposed extension, is to allow all 50 states to experiment at the state level with developing a mandatory training component of unemployment compensation. But I believe deeply, people should not get money for doing nothing.

Source: 2011 GOP Google debate in Orlando FL,
Sept. 22, 2011

Paul on Social Security Privatization

System is broke; allow young people to get out

Q: Is Social Security a Ponzi scheme?

PAUL: Well, I agree that Social Security is broke. We spent all the money and it's on its last legs unless we do something. One bill that I had in Congress—never got passed—was to prevent the Congress from spending any of that money on the wars and all the nonsense that we do around the world. Now the other thing that I would like to see done is a transition. I think it's terrible that the Social Security system has the problems it has, but if people wouldn't have spent the money we would be OK. Now, what I would like to do is to allow all the young people to get out of Social Security and go on their own. Now, the big question is, is how would the funding occur?

Source: 2011 GOP Tea Party debate in Tampa FL, Sept. 12, 2011

Gingrich on Social Security Privatization

Take Social Security off federal budget; give young a choice

You deal with Social Security as a free-standing issue. And the fact is, if you allow younger Americans to have the choice to go to a Galveston or Chilean-style personal Social Security savings account, the long-term effect on Social Security is scored by the Social Security actuary as absolutely stabilizing the system and taking care of it.

The key is there is $2.4 trillion in Social Security which should be off budget, and no president of the United States should ever again say because of some political fight in Washington, I may not be able to send you your check. That money is sitting there. That money is available. And the country ought to pay the debt it owes the people who put the money in there.

Source: 2011 CNBC GOP Primary debate in Rochester Michigan,
Nov. 9, 2011

Paul on Tax-and-Spend policies

Tax code is the symptom; spending is the problem

Q: In your tax plan, you want to close down agencies. Where do those jobs go?

A: Eventually they go into the private sector. Then don't all leave immediately when the plan goes into effect. But what my plan does is it addresses taxes in a little different way. We are talking about the tax code. But that's the consequence, that's the symptom.

The disease is spending. Every time you spend, spending is a tax. We tax the people, we borrow, and then we print the money and the prices go up, and that is a tax. So you have to address the subject of spending. That is the tax.

That is the reason I go after the spending. I propose in the first year cut $1 trillion out of the budget in 5 departments. Now the other thing is that you must do if you want to get the economy going and going again is you have to get rid of price-fixing. And the most significant price-fixing that goes on, that gave us the bubble and destroyed the economy, is the price-fixing of the Federal Reserve.

Source: 2011 CNBC GOP Primary debate in Rochester Michigan,
Nov. 9, 2011

Gingrich on Tax-and-Spend policies

1995 budget: cut taxes, regulations, & spending

After the 12-year siege of Reagan-Bush, I thought the plague of Reaganism had passed. How was I to know that a more virulent strain, personified by Newt Gingrich and the *Contract With America*, was about to lay us low? It was rolled out, like a big legislative Trojan horse, just six weeks before the congressional elections. It was fiendishly brilliant; in the end we lost 54 seats.

The guts of that Trojan horse were taken nearly verbatim from Reagan's 1985 State of the Union speech. The core of that speech, the heart of Reaganism, venerated the new Republican mantra of cutting taxes on wealth and slashing government spending on entitlement programs. "Entitlement" became identified with a newly-revised, all-purpose political scapegoat: the undeserving poor.

The massive budget cuts in the Gingrich Congress in 1995 were the cutting edge of Reagan's 1985 vision of boosting growth and balancing the budget by cutting regulation on corporations, taxes on the wealthy, and spending on the poor.

Source: A Bad Day Since, by Rep. Charles Rangel (D-NY), p. 229-30,
Aug 5, 2008

Paul on Marriage Penalty

Voted YES on reducing Marriage Tax
by $399B over 10 years

Vote to pass a bill that would reduce taxes for married people by $399.2 billion over 10 years by doubling the couples' deduction and the child tax credit. Among other provisions, the bill would allow married couples filing jointly to claim a standard deduction equal to the deduction they would receive filing singly.

Source: Bill sponsored by Weller, R–IL; Bill HR 6;
vote number 75 on March 29, 2001

NOTE: The 'Marriage Penalty' means that two people filing taxes together pay more than if they filed as two singles separately. This situation has existed in the tax code since 1969, when the tax code was reformed to account for women entering the workplace. The bill referenced above became law in June 2001 as the "Marriage Penalty and Family Tax Relief Act." It changed tax deductions and child credits to remove that aspect of the 'Marriage Penalty,' but did not address the core distinction that a couple filing jointly still pay more than the same couple filing separately.

Gingrich on Marriage Penalty

Marriage penalty costs low-income couples $4,600 per year

Americans, Gingrich believes, are not rule-dominated; they are incentive-dominated. Because of this, today's welfare incentives are backwards in a democratic, entrepreneurial society.

His favorite example: the tax code's marriage penalty, or that part that affects lower-income citizens. Gingrich used the example of a man earning $11,000 a year who wanted to marry a woman earning the same amount. Because each taxpayer would be eligible for the Earned Income Tax Credit, a marriage ceremony and license would cost the couple $4,000 a year.

"And then you have politicians," Gingrich says, "who say, 'Gee, we have too many births out of wedlock.' And your government wants to encourage you to get married by taking from you 25% of your income?"

Gingrich doesn't blame individuals for socially damaging behavior. His target is the system that fosters it. He wants instead a system that guides citizens to the proper choices.

Source: Newt!, by Dick Williams, p. 43, June 1, 1995

Paul vs. Gingrich on Social Issues

Social issues focus on matters which are based primarily on moral values, including the following topics:

- *Abortion:* including stem cells, partial birth, and state-level restrictions. This topic has always been the most viewed topic on our websitewww.OnTheIssues.org, so we explore several aspects. Paul, a medical doctor, opposes abortion on medical grounds; Gingrich opposes abortion on moral grounds.

- *Civil Rights:* including gay rights and minority rights. For the 2012 race, gay rights will dominate this category. Rep. Paul wants government out of marriage, including gay marriage, and out of running businesses, including racial hiring decisions. Rep. Gingrich would define marriage in the Constitution.

- *Education:* including college funding issues, school vouchers, and school prayer. Rep. Paul wants the federal government out of college loans, out of school funding, and out of school prayer. Rep. Gingrich has a more traditional conservative view.

- *Families and Children:* including father's rights and family values; not a key focus for either candidate.

- *Principles and Values:* including religious issues, on which Gingrich has written a book, *Rediscovering God in America.* This category includes the "revolution" aspects of both candidates: Gingrich in 1994 and Paul in 2008.

- *Welfare and Poverty:* including homelessness, welfare payments, and other poverty programs. Paul wants the federal government out of providing welfare; Gingrich wants to refocus welfare on a moral foundation.

Ron Paul on Social Issues

Newt Gingrich on Social Issues

Paul on Abortion Funding

No tax funding for organizations that promote abortion

Q: The Mexico City Policy states that as a condition for a foreign organization to receive federal funds, they will neither "perform nor actively promote abortion." The Mexico City Policy is the principle of not giving our tax dollars to organizations within our country that actively promote or provide abortions. It's an American law. Would you work to apply this Mexico City policy to organizations within the US?

BROWNBACK: This is Ronald Reagan' policy that we wouldn't use federal funds to support organizations that promote abortions overseas.

Q: I want to know, will you defund Planned Parenthood?

HUCKABEE: Yes.

TANCREDO: Yes.

COX: Yes.

BROWNBACK: Yes.

PAUL: Yes.

HUNTER: Yes.

KEYES: Yes.

Source: 2007 GOP Values Voter Presidential Debate, Sept. 17, 2007

Gingrich on Abortion Funding

Immediately cease public funding for abortion providers

Abortion is perhaps the most contentious public issue today, testing the professed American principle that every human life is precious and entitled to constitutional protection. With the advent of increasingly sophisticated ultrasound technology, public opinion on abortion has shifted, with a majority of Americans now identifying themselves as pro-life. As with any public policy, the more strongly public opinion is swayed in defense of unborn life, the more our laws should and will change as a result.

Source: A Nation Like No Other, by Newt Gingrich, p. 92, June 13, 2011

Paul on Abortion Morality

Abortion causes inconsistent moral basis for value of life

In the 1960s when abortion was still illegal, I witnessed, as an OB/GYN resident, the abortion of a fetus that weighed approximately 2 pounds. It was placed in a bucket, crying and struggling to breathe, and the medical personnel pretended not to notice. Soon the crying stopped. This harrowing event forced me to think more seriously about this important issue.

That same day in the OB suite, an early delivery occurred and the infant boy was only slightly larger than the one that was just aborted. But in this room everybody did everything conceivable to save this child's life.

My conclusion that day was that we were overstepping the bounds of morality by picking and choosing who should live and who should die. There was no consistent moral basis to the value of life under these circumstances. Some people believe that being pro-choice is being on the side of freedom. I've never understood how killing a human being, albeit a small one in a special place, is portrayed as a precious right.

Source: Liberty Defined, by Rep. Ron Paul, p. 1, April 19, 2011

Gingrich on Abortion Morality

Stop forcing pro-choice morality
on religious organizations

The campaign against public prayer and the display of religious symbols is only the tip of the iceberg. Consider the following examples:

- In May 2009, a pro-life nurse at a New York hospital was forced to participate in a late-term abortion, even though the hospital had agreed in writing to honor her religious convictions.

- In Jan. 2010, a Baptist minister was sentenced to thirty days in jail for peacefully protesting outside a Planned Parenthood abortion clinic in Oakland, California.

- In Feb. 2010, five men were threatened with arrest for preaching Christianity on a public sidewalk in Virginia.

The Founders would have regarded such efforts to remove God from public life as a fundamental threat to liberty. They saw no contradiction between the First Amendment, which was designed to *protect* religious liberty, and the need for a free people to remember that their liberties come from God.

Source: A Nation Like No Other, by Newt Gingrich, p. 87-89,
June 13, 2011

Paul on Judicial Activism

Nominate only judges who refuse
to legislate from the bench

Q: Will you nominate only judges who are demonstrably faithful to the judicial role of following only the text of the Constitution, and who not only refuse to legislate from the bench, but are committed to reversing prior court decision where activist judges strayed from the judicial role and legislated from the bench?

HUCKABEE: Yes.

TANCREDO: Yes.

COX: Yes.

BROWNBACK: Yes.

PAUL: Yes.

HUNTER: Yes.

KEYES: Yes.

Source: 2007 GOP Values Voter Presidential Debate, Sept. 17, 2007

Gingrich on Judicial Activism

Impeach judges who don't abide
by Constitution as written

There is a sense of defeatism when it comes to the federal courts because the Left-liberal media insist on judicial supremacy and assert that the only way to check and balance the courts is to pass a constitutional amendment. This is of course absurd and historically wrong. The amendment process was not intended to be the way to check and balance Supreme Court decisions. There are some steps we can take through the legislative and executive branches to reestablish a constitutional balance.

1. The American people can insist on electing Senators who promise to confirm judges who enforce the Constitution as written.

2. The legislative & executive branches can limit jurisdiction of the federal courts to hear certain types of cases where they believe the federal judiciary is wrong.

3. Americans can only insist that judges who consistently ignore the Constitution and the legitimate powers of the other two coequal branches of the federal government be considered unfit the serve and be impeached.

Source: Winning the Future, by Newt Gingrich, p. 81–84, Oct. 1, 2005

Paul on Welfare State

Welfare state isn't in the Constitution

Q: A long time ago, a fellow Texan was horrified to see young kids coming into the classroom hungry. The young student teacher later went on to be President Lyndon Johnson. Providing nutrition at schools for children—is that a role of the federal government

PAUL: Well, I'm sure, when he did that, he did it with local government, and there's no rules against that. That'd be fine. But that doesn't imply that you want to endorse the entire welfare state. No; it isn't authorized in the Constitution for us to run a welfare state. And it doesn't work. All it's filled up with is mandates. But, yes, if there are poor people in Texas, we have a responsibility—I'd like to see it as voluntary as possible—but under our Constitution, our states have that right—if they feel the obligation, they have a perfect right to. This whole idea that there's something wrong with people who don't lavish out free stuff from the federal government somehow aren't compassionate enough. I resist those accusations.

Source: 2011 GOP debate in Simi Valley CA at the Reagan Library,
Sep 7, 2011

Gingrich on Welfare State

When free welfare is provided, people choose not to work

President Lyndon Johnson famously announced the War on Poverty. From 1965 to 2008, total spending on this "war" reached nearly $16 trillion in 2008 dollars. And what did we get in return? Soon after the War on Poverty programs were adopted, the years-long decline in American poverty suddenly stopped.

By 2009 the poverty rate stood at 14.3%—about where it was when the War of Poverty began. With the government providing so much in free welfare, many people chose not to work. Welfare recipients who go to work lose their benefits as their income rises. This is effectively an extra tax on work that must be paid on top of the usual array of federal, state, and local taxes.

Source: A Nation Like No Other, by Newt Gingrich, p.109, June 13, 2011

FactCheck: Poverty rate has fallen under War on Poverty

PolitiFact.com reports: [LBJ's programs] focused on elderly poverty, which is down to 13%. [Gingrich also] uses the wrong numbers. The poverty rate was 17.3% in 1965, not 14%. So the poverty has fallen by 3 percentage points, or by about 1/6 its original level. Counting different years shows even more decline. In 1962, the poverty rate ranged was 20%. In pre-recession 2007, it stood at 12.5%. Comparing 1962 and 2007, the poverty rate dropped by over 1/3.

Source: FactCheck by PolitiFact.com, July 26, 2011

Paul on Don't-Ask-Don't-Tell

Don't ask, don't tell is a decent policy for gays in army

Q: Most of our closest allies, including Great Britain and Israel, allow gays and lesbians to openly serve in the military. Is it time to end "Don't ask, don't tell" policy and allow gays and lesbians to serve openly in the US military?

A: I think the current policy is a decent policy. And the problem that we have with dealing with this subject is we see people as groups, as they belong to certain groups and that they derive their rights as belonging to groups. We don't get our rights because we're gays or women or minorities. We get our rights from our creator as individuals. So every individual should be treated the same way. So if there is homosexual behavior in the military that is disruptive, it should be dealt with. But if there's heterosexual sexual behavior that is disruptive, it should be dealt with. So it isn't the issue of homosexuality, it's the concept and the understanding of individual rights. If we understood that, we would not be dealing with this very important problem.

Source: 2007 GOP debate at Saint Anselm College, June 3, 2007

Gingrich on Don't-Ask-Don't-Tell

Army & Marines wanted Don't-Ask-Don't-Tell

Q: Now gays are allowed to serve openly in the military; would you leave that policy in place or would you try to change it back to "don't ask/don't tell"?

CAIN: If I had my druthers, I never would have overturned "don't ask/don't tell" in the first place. Now that they have changed it, I wouldn't create a distraction trying to turn it over as president.

GINGRICH: Well, I think it's very powerful that both the Army and the Marines overwhelmingly opposed changing it, that their recommendation was against changing it. And if as president—I've met with them and they said, you know, it isn't working, it is dangerous, it's disrupting unit morale, and we should go back, I would listen to the commanders whose lives are at risk about the young men and women that they are, in fact, trying to protect.

BACHMANN: I would keep the "don't ask/don't tell" policy.

Source: 2011 GOP primary debate in Manchester NH, June 13, 2011

Paul on Defense of Marriage Act

No need for Marriage Amendment; DOMA is enough

Q: Will you support a federal marriage amendment, and what else will you do to protect the institution of marriage?

A: I think the best thing the president can do is set a good example, and I would start with having been married 50 years, and proud of it. I believe, also, that I do not see any need for another constitutional amendment. I think we have fallen into a trap that we have to redefine marriage. We're on the defensive, defining marriage. Why don't you just tell them to look it up in the dictionary, to find out what a marriage says? For federal legal purposes, the Defense of Marriage Act is proper. It takes care of all the problems. If you have to have rules and regulations, put it at the state level, like the Constitution says. But you know, marriage only came about and getting licenses only came about in recent history for health reasons. Marriage is a church function. It's not a state function. I don't think you need a license to get married.

Source: 2007 GOP Values Voter Presidential Debate, Sept. 17, 2007

NOTE: "DOMA" refers to the Defense of Marriage Act, passed by Congress in 1996, which defined marriage as consisting of one man and one woman (in other words, barring same-sex marriage). DOMA applies to all federal benefits and taxes, but not necessarily to state benefits and taxes.

Gingrich on Defense of Marriage Act

I helped author DOMA; if it fails, amend Constitution

Q: Are you a George W. Bush Republican, meaning a constitutional amendment to ban same-sex marriage, or a Dick Cheney Republican, that same sex marriage should be a state's decision?

GINGRICH: I helped author the Defense of Marriage Act which the Obama administration should be protecting in court. I think if that fails, you have no choice except a constitutional amendment.

SANTORUM: Constitutional amendment.

PAWLENTY: Constitutional amendment.

CAIN: State decision.

ROMNEY: Constitutional.

Source: 2011 GOP primary debate in Manchester NH, June 13, 2011

Paul on Churches and Same-Sex Marriage

Let churches marry couples, without government document

Q: [to Bachmann]: New Hampshire is one of five states where gays can marry legally. As president, would you try to overturn state laws?

BACHMANN: Well, I do believe in the 10th Amendment and I do believe in self-determination for the states. I also believe that marriage is between a man and a woman. I don't see that it's the role of a president to go into states and interfere with their state laws.

PAUL: The federal government shouldn't be involved. I wouldn't support an amendment. But let me suggest, get the government out of it. Why doesn't it go to the church? And why doesn't it to go to the individuals? I don't think government should give us a license to get married. It should be in the church.

Source: 2011 GOP primary debate in Manchester NH, June 13, 2011

Gingrich on Churches and Same-Sex Marriage

Stop forcing same-sex marriage
on religious organizations

The campaign against religious symbols is only the tip of the iceberg. Consider the following:

In Nov. 2006, a student at Missouri State University studying to be a social worker was interrogated by school faculty and subsequently threatened with expulsion when, after being required to lobby state legislators in favor of same-sex adoptions, she asked for an alternative assignment that did not violate her Christian beliefs.

In Oct. 2009, Congress passed a "hate speech" law subjecting pastors and other faith leaders to prosecution for preaching aspects of their faith that the state decides are "hate speech."

A Methodist camp meeting association in New Jersey now faces civil rights charges after refusing now faces civil rights charges after refusing a request to host a same-sex couple's "civil union ceremony" in its worship space.

A young Christian photographer was fined nearly $7,000 in attorney's fees after she refused to photograph the "commitment ceremony" of a same-sex couple.

Source: A Nation Like No Other, by Newt Gingrich, p. 87-88, June 13, 2011

Paul on Affirmative Action

No affirmative action for any group

All rights are individuals. We do not get our rights because we belong to a group. Whether it's homosexuals, women, minorities, it leads us astray. You don't get your rights belonging to your group. A group can't force themselves on anybody else. So there should be no affirmative action for any group.

This violates the principle on the importance of the individual, and confuses us about the importance of individual rights, which is the purpose of the Constitution. Defend our individual rights.

Source: 2007 GOP Values Voter Presidential Debate, Sept. 17, 2007

Gingrich on Affirmative Action

Affirmative action OK individually, but not by group

In 1995, a California referendum [was proposed to] eliminate affirmative action programs in state and local government. When Gingrich was asked about the issue at his regular daily press conference, he was consistent.

"It is my belief," he said, "that affirmative action programs, if done for individuals, are good, and if done by some group distinction, are bad. Because it is antithetical to the American dream to measure people by the genetic pattern of their great-grandmothers. So, I'm very interested in rewriting the affirmative action programs so that they allow individuals to get help whether they are Appalachian white or blacks from Atlanta. But I think it ought to be based on the fact that you individually have worked hard and are trying to rise and that you come out of a background of poverty and a background of cultural need."

A reporter noted that some beneficiaries of government preferences have been subjected to discrimination for centuries. "That's been true of virtually every American."

Source: Newt!, by Dick Williams, p. 31, June 1, 1995

Paul on College Loans

Student loan program is
a total failure and unconstitutional

Q: We are looking at student loan debt that is near $1 trillion. How would you make college more affordable?

PAUL: Well, I think you proved that the policy of student loans is a total failure. I mean, a trillion dollars of debt? And what have they gotten? A poorer education and costs that have skyrocketed because of inflation, and they don't have jobs. There's nothing more dramatically failing than that program. There's no authority in the Constitution for the federal government to be dealing with education. We should get rid of the loan programs. We should get rid of the Department of Education and give tax credits, if you have to, to help people.

Q: But how do they pay for it? How do they now pay for college?

PAUL: The way you pay for cellphones and computers. You have the marketplace there. There's competition. Quality goes up. The price goes down.

Source: 2011 CNBC GOP Primary debate in Rochester MI, Nov. 9, 2011

Gingrich on College Loans

College students should work and graduate with no debt

PAUL: [to Gingrich]: There's no authority in the Constitution for the federal government to be dealing with education. We should get rid of the student loan programs.

GINGRICH: The student loan program began when Lyndon Johnson announced it, I think, with a $15 million program. It's an absurdity. What does it do? It expands the ability of students to stay in college longer because they don't see the cost. It actually means they take fewer hours per semester on average. It takes longer for them to get through school. It allows them to tolerate tuitions going up absurdly.

Now, let me give you a contrast that's very startling. The College of the Ozarks is a work-study college. You have to work 20 hours a week during the year to pay tuition and books. Now, that is a model so different, it will be culture shock for the students of America to learn we actually expect them to go to class, study, get out quickly, charge as little as possible, and emerge debt free by doing the right things for 4 years.

Source: 2011 CNBC GOP Primary debate in Rochester MI, Nov. 9, 2011

Paul on Department of Education

Close Department of Education, but don't dismantle public schools

Q: You said you want to abolish the public school system.

A: We elected conservatives to get rid of the Department of Education. We used to campaign on that. And what did we do? We doubled the size. I want to reverse that trend.

Q: What about public schools? Are you still for dismantling them?

A: No, I'm not. It's not in my platform.

Q: When you ran for president in 1988, you called for the abolition of public schools.

A: I bet that's a misquote. I do not recall that.

Source: Meet the Press: 2007 "Meet the Candidates" series,
Dec 23, 2007

Gingrich on Department of Education

Dramatically shrink the federal Department of Education

Q: What as president would you seriously do about a massive overreach of big government into the classroom?

Gov. GARY JOHNSON: I am going to promise to advocate the abolishment of the federal Department of Education.

GINGRICH: I think you need very profound reform of education at the state level. You need to dramatically shrink the federal Department of Education, get rid of virtually all of its regulations. And the truth is, I believe we'd be far better off if most states adopted a program of the equivalent of Pell Grants for K-through-12, so that parents could choose where their child went to school, whether it was public, or private, or home-schooling, and parents could be involved. Florida has a virtual school program that is worth the entire country studying as an example

Source: 2011 GOP Google debate in Orlando FL, Sept. 22, 2011

Paul on School Prayer

School prayer is not a federal issue

[Limits on Constitutional authority] holds true for issues like prayer in schools. Such issues were never meant to be decided by federal judges. The whole point of the American Revolution was to vindicate the principle of local self government.

Source: The Revolution: A Manifesto, by Ron Paul, p. 61, April 1, 2008

Voted NO on allowing school prayer during the War on Terror

Children's Prayers Resolution: Expressing the sense of Congress that schools should allow children time to pray for, or silently reflect upon, the country during the war against terrorism.

Source: Bill sponsored by Rep. Isakson, R-GA; Bill H.Con.Res.239;
vote number 445 on Nov. 15, 2001

Gingrich on School Prayer

Voluntary school prayer creates bond between you and Creator

There's a reason why voluntary school prayer mattered, and the reason goes far from the concept of being endowed by our Creator and getting authority from a Supreme Being.

I had a very bright student in the class who said, "Do you really think voluntary school prayer matters that much? Why does it matter? You really think 30 seconds matter?" And I suddenly realized the reason it matters is it establishes at the beginning of the day the concept of a hierarchy. That the teacher is an intermediary between the Creator who is endowing is with our unalienable rights and us.

If there is a Creator and your rights are endowed by the Creator, then there is a direct bond between you and the Creator. Now this is not a violation of church and state. They're not

Source: Newt!, by Dick Williams, p.172-173, June 1, 1995

Paul on Homeschooling

Guarantee parity for home school diplomas

My commitment is to ensure that home schooling remains a practical alternative for American families. As President I will advance tax credits through the Family Education Freedom Act, which reduces taxes to make it easier for parents to home school by allowing them to devote more of their own funds to their children's education. I am committed to guaranteeing parity for home school diplomas and advancing equal scholarship consideration for students entering college from a home school environment.

Source: 2008 House campaign website, www.ronpaul2008.com, "Issues,"
Sept. 1, 2007

Gingrich on Homeschooling

Let parents choose public, private, parochial, or homeschool

Home-educated students score an average of 15 to 30 points higher than public-school students on standardized tests, including the SAT and ACT, regardless of their parents' level of formal education or the level of family income. Because families who homeschool do not depend on taxpayer-funded resources, taxpayers save an estimated $16 billion each year thanks to homeschooling.

Except in cases of demonstrable neglect or abuse, lawmakers and judges must enact and enforce policies that support the right of parents to direct the upbringing of their children and choose the educational model that best suits the child's needs, whether public school, private or parochial school, or homeschooling.

Source: A Nation Like No Other, by Newt Gingrich, p. 94-95,
June 13, 2011

Paul on School Vouchers

Competition helps, but vouchers invite bureaucratic control

Competition is helpful in any endeavor. And this is true in education. The near monopoly control over the indoctrination of young people in our public school systems is counterbalanced by homeschooling, private schooling and education readily available on the Internet. The regulations on starting a variety of alternatives to public schooling are extremely tight and keep the market from operating as it might.

The effort to provide more competition to the public school system has not solved the problem, though there are always a few who benefit from vouchers, tax credits, and charter schools. Too often these efforts are unfairly made available and do not eliminate the power of the state to control the curriculum. The best interim option for reform would be to give a tax credit for all educational expenses. Vouchers invite bureaucratic control of their usage and are unfairly distributed.

Source: Liberty Defined, by Rep. Ron Paul, p. 78-79, April 19, 2011

Gingrich on School Vouchers

Voucherize inner-city programs from schools to groceries

In a speech in March, 1995, to business leaders in suburban Atlanta, Gingrich noted that the public school system in the District of Columbia spends $9,600 a year per pupil, nearly double the national average. He suggested that for such a high level of spending, each could have private tutors and personal transportation to school—plus lunch. He advocates vouchers to parents so they can choose the schools, public or private, their children will attend.

"I think we ought to voucherize every program in the inner city with cash payments to parents allowing them to decide where and what to purchase, be it an elementary school, health care, or groceries." Some in his audience thought he was exaggerating to make a point. In a later interview, he was willing to go even further. "Suppose you need to get children away from failed teachers. What if we called on the home-schoolers in Maryland and Virginia to come to D.C. for a massive home schooling program, teaching parents how to teach their children."

Source: Newt!, by Dick Williams, p. 51-52, June 1, 1995

Paul on the Tea Party

Breaks one-day fundraising record:
$6M at "Boston Tea Party"

Ron Paul raised an astounding $6 million & change Sunday. The campaign announced they had eclipsed the $5.7 million that John Kerry raised the day after he locked up the 2004 Democratic nomination—arguably the largest single-day fundraising haul in US political history.

Paul, whose campaign has been embraced by a zealous community of online supporters, raised $4.2 million on Nov. 5, [corresponding with Guy Fawkes Day]. The current fundraising effort was timed for the 234th anniversary of the Boston Tea Party, a day meant to resonate with the Libertarian sensibilities of his supporters.

The man who engineered it—Trevor Lyman, a 37-year-old music promoter—has no official ties to the campaign and had no political experience before he engineered the innovative model for Nov. 5. He set up a website that solicited pledges for contributions to be made directly to the Paul campaign on that day—a technique that became known as a "money bomb," which he used again to such great effect Sunday.

Source: USA Today, Dec. 17, 2007

Gingrich on the Tea Party

Tea Party prevents mistake of
electing conservative Democrats

Q: What role do you think the Tea Party will play in the 2012 elections?

A: Tea Party will help prevent Republicans from making same mistakes of 2004 and 2006 & help elect conservative democrats. The most important role for the Tea Party is not in elections, but in developing local solutions as we move power out of Washington. Permanently ending the age of big government will be hard work and require a team effort between federal, state & local government.

Source: 2011 Republican primary debate on Twitter.com, July 21, 2011

Paul on Principles of Liberty

Liberty promotes peace, and peace promotes prosperity

If you follow the Constitution, you will defend freedom. Freedom brings people together. It allows people to run their lives as they choose, it allows them to practice religion as they choose, it is not confrontational & not antagonistic. The welfare state, the warfare state, & the socialist state, is exactly the opposite. It divides us, because they take away our wealth, they control it in Washington.

What is happening today? Millions of dollars of campaign funds & PAC money, and lobbying efforts to control the money that gravitates to Washington, DC. The pie is shrinking, and the people are getting angry, and we have forgotten what a free country is all about.

We've lost our confidence, because we have to have safety nets here and safety nets here and do all of these things. It's coming to an end and there's a wonderful, beautiful answer. It comes in our traditions and it comes in the principles of liberty. If you promote liberty, liberty promotes peace. And peace promotes prosperity.

Source: Speeches to 2008 Conservative Political Action Conference,
Feb. 7, 2008

Gingrich on Principles of Liberty

Five habits of liberty sustain American Exceptionalism

Looking through 400 years of American history, we find five habits of liberty that have been crucial to sustaining American Exceptionalism.

They are: faith and family, work, civil society, rule of law, and safety and peace.

Tempering man's worst impulses, these distinctly American habits are vital to cultivating an engaged, informed citizenry, which is needed to sustain a free republic and secure the unalienable rights asserted in the Declaration of Independence. The emphasis on these habits set America apart from its European counterparts, where monarchs were intent on cultivating passive, obedient subjects unlikely to change their ruler's claim to power.

Source: A Nation Like No Other, by Newt Gingrich, p. 42, June 13, 2011

Paul vs. Gingrich
on International Issues

International issues focus on foreign relations and anything involving foreign nations, including the following topics:

- *Energy and Oil:* including global warming, domestic drilling and alternative energy sources. Rep. Paul focuses on avoiding international government and reducing federal government involvement. Rep. Gingrich focuses on domestic production.

- *Free Trade:* including NAFTA (the North American Free trade Agreement) and other bilateral agreements, plus opinions on the trade organizations like the WTO (World Trade Organization). Paul wants open trade with China; Gingrich prefers protected trade.

- *Immigration:* including border security; the border fence; and dealing with the current 12 million illegal immigrants in the US. Paul focuses on realistic methods of dealing with millions of illegal aliens; Gingrich focuses on enforcement and regrets having supported Reagan's amnesty.

- *Foreign Policy:* Paul wants to reduce foreign aid and foreign entanglements. Gingrich supports "American Exceptionalism"— the topic of another Gingrich book, *A Nation Like No Other*— which Paul considers "American Imperialism."

- *Homeland Security:* this category concerns defense policy, not war policy. This category includes defense spending issues; and defense strategy goals. This is the most dramatic distinction between the two candidates: Paul wants dramatic decreases in defense spending; Gingrich wants dramatic increases.

- *War and Peace:* including the current ongoing wars in Iraq and Afghanistan. Gingrich talks tough on those, plus Iran, Korea, and Islam. Paul would withdraw from all foreign aggression.

Ron Paul
on International Issues

Newt Gingrich
on International Issues

Paul on Climate Change

Absurd to let global bureaucrats
try to manipulate climate

Regardless of whether one believes global warming is real, I seriously doubt the capacity of a global body made up of bureaucrats and scientists on the public payroll, when given the power to attempt a global climate manipulation, to cook up a workable plan with effects that cannot be discerned for twenty or more years. I've seen how government programs work. They aren't designed to last more than a single election cycle.

The idea that government can plan weather patterns for decades strikes me as the height of absurdity. Building up fear and manipulating people into demanding that government save is how radical environmentalists operate. Cap and trade legislation will introduce a whole new product of CO_2 permits that will be created and traded by the big financial interests bailed out after the crash, such as Goldman Sachs.

Source: Liberty Defined, by Rep. Ron Paul, p.133–136, April 19, 2011

NOTE: "Cap-and-Trade" refers to a carbon dioxide (CO_2) emissions policy where the amount of CO_2 is "capped" at a government-specified emission amount, and then the right to emit CO_2 is "traded" via emission permits. A similar program was used successfully to battle acid rain via sulfur dioxide emission permits trading on the Chicago Mercantile Exchange.

Gingrich on Climate Change

Kyoto treaty is bad for the environment and bad for America

Kyoto is a bad treaty. It is bad for the environment and it is bad for America. It sets standards that will require massive investments by the US but virtually no investments by other countries. The Senate was right when it voted unanimously against the treaty. We should insist on revisiting the entire Kyoto process and resolutely reject efforts to force us into an anti-American, environmentally failed treaty.

The US should support substantial research into climate science, managing the response to climate change, & in developing new non-carbon energy systems. It is astounding to watch people blithely propose trillions of dollars in spending on a topic on which we have failed to spend modest amounts to better understand.

It is astounding to have people focus myopically on carbon as the sole source of climate change. The world's climate has changed in the past with sudden speed and dramatic impact. Global warming may happen. On the other hand it is possible Europe will experience another ice age.

Source: Gingrich Communications website, www.newt.org, Dec. 1, 2006

NOTE: "Kyoto" refers to a Climate Change Treaty which sets carbon dioxide reduction targets for the US and other developed countries. Completed in 1998, the US has not yet signed. This is politically controversial because it would require the US to cut CO_2 emissions, which is potentially costly.

Paul on Oil Drilling

Big Oil profits ok; Big Oil subsidies are not

Q: Bush's energy bill provided billions of dollars in tax breaks & subsidies to the oil companies with the goal of boosting domestic production at a time of record profits. Do you support that?

A: I don't think the profits is the issue. The profits are okay if they're legitimately earned in a free market. What I object to are subsidies to big corporations when we subsidize them and give them R&D money. I don't think that should be that way. They should take it out of the funds that they earn.

Source: 2007 GOP debate at Saint Anselm College, June 3, 2007

Gingrich on Oil Drilling

2008 book: Drill Here, Drill Now, Pay Less

In 2008, American Solutions launched an online petition drive to demand Congress lift the 25-year-old moratorium on new offshore drilling. We collected 1.5 million signatures. Our effort sparked a nationwide grassroots rebellion that resulted in Congress allowing the moratorium to expire.

I wrote a book in fall 2008 called "Drill Here, Drill Now, Pay Less," describing America's vast energy potential and explain how misguided government policies have prevented us from becoming an energy powerhouse.

Source: Real Change, by Newt Gingrich, p.205-206, Dec. 18, 2007

2008 petition drive: Drill here, Drill now, Pay less

In 2008 when gasoline was at $4 a gallon, American Solutions launched a petition drive: Drill here, Drill now, Pay less.

The Left couldn't survive in a world where we had the courage to say, "Why don't we find American oil and why don't we find American gas, and why don't we have the next building boom in the United States, not in Dubai. And why don't we make sure that the terrorists run out of money?" And that ought to be our approach to this, so let's do it now.

First of all: Reopen off of Louisiana. The people of Louisiana want it to happen. So let's reopen the areas off only those states that want to reopen them. Let's let them do it now.

Source: Speech at Conservative Political Action Conference, Feb. 11, 2011

Paul on China Trade

China trade not contingent on human rights & product safety

Q: Sarah Lu was forced to work in labor camps for six years, for the crime of being a Christian house church leader. Thousands of prisoners of conscience are forced to manufacture items that stock our American shelves. Would you make future trade with China contingent on them measurably improving their record on religious freedom & human rights?

HUCKABEE: Yes.

TANCREDO: Yes.

COX: Yes.

BROWNBACK: Yes.

PAUL: No.

HUNTER: Absolutely. Yes. Good question.

KEYES: Yes.

Source: 2007 GOP Values Voter Presidential Debate, Sept. 17, 2007

Gingrich on China Trade

Protectionism helps China & India
challenge US supremacy

In the US, there exists a coalition of union leaders who prefer protection over competition. This liberal coalition complains about companies' outsourcing jobs while insisting on corporate taxes that encourage companies to go overseas. They prefer that government impose on business obsolete, absurd work rules, even though these raise costs, lower productivity, and make America less competitive in the world market.

The challenge to American economic supremacy from 1.3 billion Chinese and more than 1.1 billion Indians is vastly greater than anything we have previously seen. India's embrace of capitalism and China's bizarre combination of Marxist-Leninist government and free market initiatives will create a future where one-fourth of the world's markets will be controlled by these countries. Those who advocate economic isolationism and protectionism are advocating a policy that could help China and India surpass the US in economic power in our children's or grandchildren's lifetime.

Source: Gingrich Communications website, www.newt.org, Dec. 1, 2006

Paul on National ID Cards

Tamper-proof I.D. for immigrants is a bad idea

I get a little bit worried when we talk about the tamper-proof I.D. for illegals or immigrants, because how do you do that? Anybody that is an immigrant or looks like an immigrant would have to have an I.D. And then, you can't discriminate, so everybody's going to have the I.D. I think it's opening the door for the national I.D., and we should be very, careful about that.

Source: 2008 Facebook/WMUR-NH Republican primary debate,
Jan 5, 2006

Gingrich on National ID Cards

Employers should use e-verify for all hires

Q: Should we make all businesses use E-Verify, a government database, to check whether or not new hires are illegal? Or would that turn small businessmen into immigration agents?

GINGRICH: Well, let me say, first of all, I think we would be better off to outsource E-Verify to American Express, MasterCard or Visa, because they actually know how to run a program like that without massive fraud. Second, the program should be as easy as swiping your credit card when you buy gasoline. And so I would ask of employers, what is it you would object to in helping the US in dealing with the problem involving illegal immigration?

Q: Would you support each state enforcing the immigration laws since the federal government is not?

GINGRICH: I strongly favor 100% control of the border, and I strongly favor English as the official language of government. I favor modernizing the legal visa system. We have a terribly antiquated legal system while our border is too open for people who are illegal.

Source: 2011 GOP Google debate in Orlando FL, Sept. 22, 2011

Paul on Illegal Alien Deportation

No amnesty, but impractical to round up 12 million illegals

Q: Is it even practical to try to send 12 million illegal immigrants all home?

A: I would not sign a bill like [comprehensive immigration reform], because it would be amnesty. I also think that it's pretty impractical to get an army in this country to round up 12 or maybe 20 million. But I do believe that we have to stick to our guns on obeying the law, and anybody who comes in here illegally shouldn't be rewarded. And that would be the case.

Source: 2007 GOP Presidential Forum at Morgan State University,
Sep 27, 2007

No amnesty, but border fence isn't so important

Q: You voted to support that 700-mile fence along the border with Mexico. Is there a need for a similar fence along the border with Canada?

PAUL: No. The fence was my weakest reason for voting for that, but enforcing the law was important, and border security is important. And we've talked about amnesty, which I'm positively opposed to. If you subsidize something, you get more of it. We subsidize illegal immigration, we reward it by easy citizenship, either birthright or amnesty.

Source: 2007 GOP debate at Saint Anselm College, June 3, 2007

Gingrich on Illegal Alien Deportation

Review all illegal aliens & if you have no ties, go home

Q: Back in the '80s, you voted for legislation that had a pathway to citizenship for illegal immigrants. Some called it amnesty then; they still call it amnesty now. What would you do if you were President, with these millions of illegal immigrants, many of whom have been in this country for a long time?

GINGRICH: Let me start and just say I think that we ought to have an H-1 visa that goes with every graduate degree in math, science and engineering so that people stay here. I did vote for the Simpson-Mazzoli Act. I believe ultimately you have to find some system that reviews the people who are here. If you've come here recently, you have no ties to this country, you ought to go home. If you've been here 25 years and you got three kids and two grandkids, you've been paying taxes and obeying the law, you belong to a local church, I don't think we're going to separate you from your family, uproot you forcefully and kick you out.

Source: 2011 CNN National Security GOP primary debate, Nov. 22, 2011

NOTE: The "Simpson-Mazzoli Act" refers to the Immigration Reform and Control Act of 1986, was the immigration reform supported by President Reagan. Its opponents claimed that it granted amnesty in exchange for tightening immigration law, but that the tightening never occurred while the amnesty did.

Paul on Guest Workers

Give illegals limbo status: a green card with an asterisk

Immigrants who can't be sent back due to the magnitude of the problem should not be given citizenship—no amnesty should be granted. Maybe a "green card" with an asterisk could be issued. This in-between status, keeping illegal immigrants in limbo, will be said that it will create a class of 2nd-class citizens. Yet it could be argued that it may well allow some immigrants who come here illegally a beneficial status without automatic citizenship—a much better option than deportation.

Source: Liberty Defined, by Rep. Ron Paul, p.156, April 19, 2011

Voted YES on more immigrant visas for skilled workers

Vote to pass a bill to increase the number of temporary visas granted to highly skilled workers from 65,000 to 115,000 by the year 2000.

Source: Bill introduced by Smith, R–TX.; Bill HR 3736;
vote number 460 on Sept. 24, 1998

Gingrich on Guest Workers

I voted for Reagan's legal guest worker program

Q: Your current perception on immigration reform is a little different on your initial positions under Reagan?

GINGRICH: I think we have to find a way to get to a country in which everybody who's here is here legally. But you referenced President Reagan. In 1986, I voted for the Simpson-Mazzoli Act, which in fact did grant some amnesty in return for promises. President Reagan wrote in his diary that year that he signed the act because we were going to control the border and we were going to have an employer program where it was a legal guest worker program. That's in his diary. I'm with President Reagan. We ought to control the border, we ought to have a legal guest worker program. We ought to outsource it, frankly, to American Express, Visa, and MasterCard, so there's no counterfeiting, which there will be with the federal government. We should be very tough on employers once you have that legal program.

Source: 2011 GOP debate in Simi Valley CA at the Reagan Library,
Sep 7, 2011

Paul on American Exceptionalism

Exceptionalism shouldn't mean using force around the world

There's been talk lately about American exceptionalism; it's been the greatest country, most freedom, most prosperity. My concern is I'm afraid we're losing it, I'm afraid we've given up on our devotion to liberty, that's where our problem is. But where I think we go astray on this exceptionalism is there are some people and sometimes they're referred as neoconservatives and they're sort of neo-Jacobins where they believe that we have this moral responsibility to use force to go around the world and say "you will do it our way or else." Well, force doesn't work; it never works.

The best way to get people to act more like us if we're doing a good job, is for us to have a sound economy, a sound dollar, treat people decently, have a foreign policy that makes common sense, treat people like we want to be treated, and then maybe they would want to emulate us and say "freedom does work and we ought to try it." But we can't force it on other people.

Source: Speech at 2011 Conservative Political Action Conference,
Feb 11, 2011

NOTE: "American exceptionalism" means that America has a unique status in the world today. The interest in American exceptionalism counters Obama's rejection of the concept, when Obama said, "Sure, I believe in American exceptionalism in the same way the British believe in British exceptionalism and the Greeks believe in Greek exceptionalism." Republicans generally interpret that as meaning, "No, I don't believe in your version of American exceptionalism at all."

Gingrich on American Exceptionalism

American Exceptionalism:
uniquely far-reaching individualism

American Exceptionalism starts with the idea of a uniquely insistent and far-reaching individualism. It's a view of the individual person which gives unprecedented weight to his or her choices, interests, and claims.

I think this is at the core of the American idea, at the core of the American sense of who we are. That we are uniquely individuals, and that each person is endowed by their Creator, every man, every woman, every child, is endowed by their Creator with inalienable rights. That's a very important concept. They cannot be alienated from you, they're yours, they're bound to you, and therefore, the system has to be built around your rights unless you voluntarily loan some of them to the state.

Notice how different that is from all historic experiences where the government, the king, or the dictator is empowered by God or by history in the Marxist model."

Source: Newt!, by Dick Williams, p. 15, June 1, 1995

Paul on North Korea

Get out of South Korea and let two Koreas unify

Q: Under President Paul, if North Korea invaded South Korea, would we respond?

A: Why should we unless the Congress declared war? I mean, why are we there? In South Korea, they're begging and pleading to unify their country, and we get in their way. They want to build bridges and go back and forth. Vietnam, we left under the worst of circumstances. The country is unified. They have become Westernized. We trade with them. Their president comes here. And Korea, we stayed there and look at the mess. I mean, the problem still exists, and it's drained trillion dollars over these last 50 years. We can't afford it anymore. We're going bankrupt. All empires end because the countries go bankrupt, and the currency crashes. That's what happening. And we need to come out of this sensibly rather than waiting for a financial crisis.

Source: Meet the Press: 2007 "Meet the Candidates" series,
Dec 23, 2007

Gingrich on North Korea

We have failed for a decade to deal with North Korea & Iran

Q: Do you believe high defense spending is essential to security?

GINGRICH: I think we are at the edge of an enormous crisis in national security. I think that we are greatly underestimating the threat to this country. And I think that the day after we celebrated the 10th anniversary of 9/11 we should be reminded exactly what is at stake if a foreign terrorist gets a nuclear weapon into this country. We have failed for a decade to deal with North Korea. We have failed for a decade to deal with Iran. We need, frankly, to ask for a very serious national dialogue.

I'd like to see Congress holding hearings on three levels of security. What do you do in Mexico where there's a civil war underway next door to us? What do you do in the Middle East where we have totally underestimated the scale of the threat? And what do you do about our national domestic industrial base which is crucial if we're going to be competitive with China? All three of those are a major threat to us.

Source: 2011 GOP Tea Party debate in Tampa FL, Sept. 12, 2011

Paul on Iranian Sanctions

Israel won't attack Iran, and neither should we

Q: If Israel attacked Iran to prevent Tehran from getting nuclear weapons, would you help?

CAIN: If Israel had a credible plan that it appeared as if they could succeed, I would support Israel, yes.

PAUL: I wouldn't do that, because I don't expect it to happen. A Mossad leader said it would be the stupidest thing to do in the world. They're not about to do this. And you're supposing that if it did, why does Israel need our help? We need to get out of their way. When they want to have peace treaties, we tell them what they can do because we buy their allegiance and they sacrifice their sovereignty to us. And then they decide they want to bomb something, that's their business, but they should suffer the consequences. When they bombed the Iraqi nuclear site, back in the '80s, I was one of the few in Congress that said it's none of our business and Israel should take care of themselves. Why do we have this automatic commitment that we're going to send our kids and send our money endlessly to Israel?

Source: 2011 CNN National Security GOP primary debate Nov. 22, 2011

Gingrich on Iranian Sanctions

Sabotage Iran's oil refinery

PERRY: [to Gingrich]: We need to sanction the Iranian Central Bank. That will shut down that economy.

GINGRICH: We ought to have a massive all-sources energy program, designed to literally replace the Iranian oil. Now that's how we won World War II. We all get sucked into these tactical discussions. We need a strategy of defeating and replacing the current Iranian regime with minimum use of force. But if we were serious, we could break the Iranian regime, I think, within a year, starting candidly with cutting off the gasoline supply to Iran, and then, frankly, sabotaging the only refinery they have.

Q: But sanctions on the Iranian Central Bank now, is that a good idea or a bad idea?

GINGRICH: I think it's a good idea if you're serious about stopping them. I think replacing the regime before they get a nuclear weapon without a war beats replacing the regime with war, which beats allowing them to have a nuclear weapon. Those are your three choices.

Source: 2011 CNN National Security GOP primary debate Nov. 22, 2011

Paul on International Diplomacy

Right to spread our values, but wrong to spread by force

Q: President Bush said in his second inaugural address, "It is the policy of the US to seek and support the growth of democratic movements and institutions in every nation and culture." Has President Bush's policy been a success?

A: Our responsibility is to spread democracy here, make sure that we have it. This is a philosophic and foreign policy problem, because what the president was saying was just a continuation of Woodrow Wilson's "making the world safe for democracy." There's nothing wrong with spreading our values around the world, but it is wrong to spread it by force. We should spread it by setting an example and going and doing a good job here. Threatening Pakistan and threatening Iran makes no sense whatsoever. I supported going after Al Qaida into Afghanistan—but, lo & behold, the neocons took over. They forgot about Bin Laden. And what they did, they went into nation-building, not only in Afghanistan, they went unjustifiably over into Iraq. And that's why we're in this mess today.

Source: 2007 GOP Iowa Straw Poll debate, Aug. 5, 2007

Gingrich on International Diplomacy

We need a dramatically expanded use of statecraft

Sen. DODD: Why aren't we using statecraft? What's happened to the utilization of other tools available to us—our economic, our political, our diplomatic resources—which are almost been neglected in this entire process?

GINGRICH: I partially agree with Sen. Dodd. I am not comfortable either with the current situation in Iraq, nor am I comfortable around the world with our extraordinarily limited use of statecraft. The North Koreans are cheating on their agreement on nuclear weapons. We still do not have control of Waziristan in northwest Pakistan, where Bin Laden's probably hiding. We have been told by the UN that the Iranians are now producing at least 1300 centrifuges, producing nuclear material, and that they almost certainly will have a nuclear weapon within a year. You look around the world, the forces of freedom are on retreat, the forces that are anti-freedom, pro-dictatorship, and, in some cases, purely evil are on offense. We need a dramatically expanded ability to use statecraft.

Source: Meet the Press: 2007 "Meet the Candidates" series,
May 20, 2007

Paul on Foreign Aid

Foreign aid wastes billions,
with unintended consequences

Believing foreign aid benefits our national security allows for billions of dollars to be wasted, encouraging a foreign policy that inevitably leads to unintended consequences that come back to haunt us. Foreign aid support comes for various reasons. Some argue we are obligated to financially support those countries that yield to our demand that we maintain military bases in their country.

American citizens are taxed to fund these foreign giveaway programs. That means funds are taken out of the hands of private citizens. Allowing government or bureaucratic decisions on spending capital is always inferior to private companies and people deciding how the money should be spent. But most importantly, foreign aid never works to achieve the stated goal of helping the poor of other nations. In poor countries food aid becomes a tool for maintaining political power. Many of the large foreign aid grants are driven strictly by special interest politics and a pretense that it serves our national security.

Source: Liberty Defined, by Rep. Ron Paul, p.118-119, April 19, 2011

Gingrich on Foreign Aid

1993: $1.6B Russia aid package
was "great defining moment"

In March 1993, I got an assistance program I could support: $1.6 billion in direct aid to help Russia stabilize.

Although a public poll said that 75% of the American people were opposed to giving Russia more money, and we were already in a hard fight for the economic plan, I felt we had no choice but to press ahead. American had spent trillions of dollars in defense to win the Cold War; we couldn't risk reversal over less than $2 billion and a bad poll. To the surprise of my staff, the congressional leaders, including the Republicans, agreed with me. At a meeting I convened to push the plan, Senator Joe Biden, the chairman of the Foreign Relations Committee, strongly endorsed the aid package.

Newt Gingrich was passionately in favor of helping Russia, saying it was a "great defining moment" for American and we had to do the right thing. Newt was trying to "out-Russia" me, which I was only too happy to have him do.

Source: My Life, by Bill Clinton, p.506-507, June 21, 2004

Paul on the Patriot Act

The Patriot Act is unpatriotic; it undermines our liberty

GINGRICH: [to Paul]: I would not change the PATRIOT Act. And I'd look at strengthening it, because I think the dangers are literally that great.

PAUL: I think the Patriot Act is unpatriotic because it undermines our liberty. I'm concerned, as everybody is, about the terrorist attack. Timothy McVeigh was a vicious terrorist. He was arrested. Terrorism is still on the books, internationally and nationally, it's a crime and we should deal with it. We dealt with it rather well with McVeigh.

GINGRICH: Timothy McVeigh succeeded. That's the whole point.

PAUL: Why I really fear it is we have drifted into a condition that we were warned against because our early founders were very clear. They said, don't be willing to sacrifice liberty for security. Today it seems too easy that our government is so willing to give up our liberties for security. I have a personal belief that you never have to give up liberty for security. You can still provide security without sacrificing our Bill of Rights.

Source: 2011 CNN National Security GOP primary debate, Nov. 22, 2011

Gingrich on the Patriot Act

Defend America & allies with information policies

We must implement policies that will ensure America's leadership, safety, and prosperity. To achieve this future we will defend America and our allies from those who would destroy us. To achieve security, we will develop the intelligence, diplomatic, information, defense, and homeland security systems and resources for success.

Source: Gingrich Communications website, www.newt.org, Dec. 1, 2006

All of us will be in danger for the rest of our lives

I think looking at [terrorism] carefully [we should] extend [the PATRIOT Act] and build an honest understanding that all of us will be in danger for the rest of our lives. This is not going to end in the short run. And we need to be prepared to protect ourselves from those who, if they could, would not just kill us individually, but would take out entire cities.

Source: 2011 CNN National Security GOP primary debate, Nov. 22, 2011

Paul on Defense spending

We can blow up the world 20 times and we can't cut a penny?

Sen. RICK SANTORUM: [to Paul]: I would absolutely not cut one penny out of military spending. We should have all the resources in place to make sure that we can defend our borders, that we can make sure that when we engage in foreign countries, we do so to succeed. The central threat right now is Iran.

PAUL: Well, I think we're on economic suicide if we're not even willing to look at some of these overseas expenditures, 900 bases, 150 different countries. We have enough weapons to blow up the world about 20-25 times. We have more weapons than all the other countries put together essentially. And we want to spend more and more, and you can't cut a penny? I mean, this is why we're at an impasse. I want to hear somebody up here willing to cut something. Something real. This budget is in bad shape and the financial calamity is going to be much worse than anybody ever invading this country. Which country is going to invade this country? They can't even shoot a missile at us.

Source: GOP 2011 primary debate in Las Vegas, Oct. 18, 2011

Gingrich on Defense spending

Defense as percentage of GDP is lowest since WWII

Q: How do you weigh the cost of fighting the war on terror against the exploding debt crisis?

Gingrich: The exploding debt crisis is because of exploding politician spending in Washington, not because of national security.

Sen. Rick Santorum: The first priority of the federal government is to keep America safe. I would not cut defense—freeze it; cut waste; and then plow savings back into Defense.

Gov. Gary Johnson: The debt is the greatest threat to national security we face today. Besides, we do not need 60,000 to 100,000 troops in Afghanistan and Iraq to protect ourselves. Nor do we need nation-building.

Gingrich: We spend less on defense today as percentage of GDP than at any time since Pearl Harbor.

Santorum: The first priority of the federal government is to keep America safe. I would not cut defense—freeze it; cut waste; and then plow savings back into Defense.

Gingrich: Controlling the border and defending America are job #1 under the Constitution.

Source: 2011 Republican primary debate on Twitter.com, July 21, 2011

Paul on Sources of Terrorism

We believe Osama's threats, so why not believe his reasons?

We believe bin Laden when he takes credit for an attack on the West, & we believe him when he warns us of an impending attack. But we refuse to listen to his explanations of why he & his allies are at war with us.

Bin Laden's claims are straightforward The US defiles Islam with military bases on holy land in Saudi Arabia, its initiation of war against Iraq, and its dollars and weapons being used against the Palestinians as the Palestinian territory shrinks and Israel's occupation expands. There will be no peace for the next 50 years or longer if we refuse to believe why those who are attacking are doing it.

To dismiss terrorism as the result of Muslims hating us because we're free is one of the greatest foreign-policy frauds ever perpetuated. Because the media and government have restated it so many times, the majority now accept it at face value. And the administration gets the political cover it needs to pursue a holy war for democracy against the infidels who hate us for our goodness.

Source: House speech, in Foreign Policy of Freedom, p.246, Jan. 29, 2003

Gingrich on Sources of Terrorism

The "Irreconcilable Wing of Islam"
threatens our way of life

Beyond the Petraeus Report, we need a report on the larger war with the Irreconcilable Wing of Islam. This enemy is irreconcilable with the modern civilized world because its values would block any woman from being in this room, having a job, voting, being education. It is irreconcilable because it cannot tolerate other religions or other lifestyles. It represents what some have called an Islamofascist approach to imposing its views on others and as such it is a moral threat to our way of life, to freedom, and to the rule of law.

The Irreconcilable Wing of Islam has emerged as an extremist movement against not only non-Muslims but also against moderate Muslims who wish both to preserve their faith and to be a part of the modern world.

Source: Real Change, by Newt Gingrich, p.292, Dec. 18, 2007

Paul on Iraq War

The Iraq war was not worth the price in blood and treasure

Q: Was the war a good idea and worth the price in blood and treasure?

A: It was a very bad idea, and it wasn't worth it. The al Qaeda wasn't there then; they're there now. There were no weapons of mass destruction. Had nothing to do with 9/11. There was no aggression. This decision on policy was made in 1998 because they called for the removal of Saddam Hussein. It wasn't worth it, and it's a sad story because we started that war and we should never be a country that starts war needlessly.

Source: 2008 GOP debate in Boca Raton Florida, Jan. 24, 2008

War in Iraq was senseless invasion of sovereign state

The war in Iraq was one of the most ill-considered, poorly planned and just plain unnecessary military conflicts in American history, and I opposed it from the beginning.

Source: The Revolution: A Manifesto, by Ron Paul, p. 21, April 1, 2008

Gingrich on Iraq War

Goal was to liberate Iraq from Saddam, not to occupy

No one in the initial war planning expected the US would try to run Iraq after defeating Saddam. There was a general belief that portions of the Iraqi army could be converted in to a policing force.

It was vital from day one that the US be seen as a liberator and not as an occupier. For some reason the lesson learned in Afghanistan—of liberating and not occupying—did not get across. Like most bureaucracies, this one looked after itself. It created a green zone of protection and comfort to shield the bureaucrats. By creating a green zone, it acknowledged that the entire rest of the country was a red zone, a danger zone. Worst of all, the decision to have an explicitly American administrator of Iraq guaranteed that America's role would change from liberator to occupier.

By Dec. 2003, things were so bad that I went public and declared that we had "gone off a cliff" in the June decisions, and that until they were reversed things were just going to get worse.

Source: Real Change, by Newt Gingrich, p.110-111, Dec. 18, 2007

Book Reviews

OnTheIssues excerpts political books and debates as the primary source of the materials in this book. Following are four book reviews, plus links online to additional books and debates cited in this book.

Book reviews:

Additional book excerpts online:

Saving Lives and Saving Money, by Newt Gingrich (2003)
www.OnTheIssues.org/Saving_Lives.htm

A Foreign Policy of Freedom, by Ron Paul (2001)
www.OnTheIssues.org/Foreign_Freedom.htm

Lessons Learned the Hard Way, by Newt Gingrich (1998)
www.OnTheIssues.org/The_Hard_Way.htm

Newt! The 2nd American Revolution, by Dick Williams (1995)
www.OnTheIssues.org/Newt_Revolution.htm

Freedom Under Siege, by Ron Paul (1987 & 2007)
www.OnTheIssues.org/Freedom_Under_Siege.htm

Book Review:
Liberty Defined:
50 Essential Issues
That Affect Our Freedom
by Rep. Ron Paul (April 19, 2011)

This book is Ron Paul's attempt to communicate libertarian ideas to his large group of followers, many of whom are new to libertarianism. It catalogs key concepts in alphabetical order, with a few pages dedicated to everything from Abortion to Zionism. Presumably the intent is that Paul's followers have a handy reference in which to look up his views, and the general libertarian view, on key issues of the 2012 presidential race.

Rep. Paul describes the book in the introduction: "The idea of this book is not to provide a blueprint for the future or an all-encompassing defense of a libertarian program. What I offer here are... not final answers but rather guideposts for thinking seriously about these topics." (p. xvii)

Paul extends in this book beyond the typical policy prescriptions about current issues and into libertarian philosophy and history. OnTheIssues covers the current issues in our excerpts below, so we'll review here some of the books' philosophical topics, which include:

Austrian Economics: A review of the 19th century philosophy underlying much of today's free-market economic outlook.

Demagogues: The bad guys in the bipartisanship debate, focusing on the "despicable" Pledge of Allegiance and flag-burning issues rampant among Republican demagogues. There's also a chapter on bipartisanship, which Paul doesn't like (a failure of bipartisanship means fewer bad laws).

Empire: Rep. Paul outlines the dangers of military over-extension from the Roman Empire and connects that to the current American Empire. Throughout the book, Rep. Paul tosses in statistics about

American imperialism and world-wide militarism (another of his big differentiators from mainstream Republicans) such as "Wars and exterminations in the 20th century reached 262 million people killed by their own governments" (p. 107)

Keynesianism: This is the philosophical opposite of Austrian Economics, and is the current underlying philosophy of Bush's & Obama's economic stimulus package,

Noble Lie: How politicians justify doing whatever they want, by claiming it's good for the country. George W. Bush's advisers fall heavily under this rubric, following Adolf Hitler and others. Julian Assange, the founder of WikiLeaks, is the hero of this chapter, since he exposed the Noble Lies of the U.S. government.

The book was written in anticipation of Rep. Paul's entry into the presidential race, released in early 2011. Paul was the Internet darling of the 2008 race, and the 2012 race is shaping up with the same following. That means thousands of young people will discover Ron Paul and will read this book for a fuller introduction to libertarianism. The approach is self-standing essays of just-a-few-pages-at-a-time, instead of a fully-involved book.

Ron Paul has plenty of fully-involved books for when his followers want yet more (as they always do). For the hardier Paulie, End the Fed, published in 2010, provides substantially more detail about the Federal Reserve and the economic situation.

Book review written Aug. 2011;
full excerpts available online at:
www.ontheissues.org/Liberty_Defined.htm

Book Review:
A Nation Like No Other:
Why American Exceptionalism Matters
by Speaker Newt Gingrich
(June 13, 2011)

The concept of "American Exceptionalism" will permeate the 2011-2012 GOP primary, and likely the 2012 general election as well. Newt Gingrich attempts to out-exception his GOP rivals here, by dedicating an entire book to the concept. We surveyed our non-pundit readers and discovered that the term itself has not yet entered the general voter lexicon—so we will first define it and then analyze its implications here, in anticipation of its usage in upcoming debates.

American exceptionalism means that America has a unique status in the world today, as the sole superpower, and that U.S. policy should work towards recognizing and maintaining that unique status. In contrast to previous nations which ruled the world, America is non-imperialist: previous nations ruled "empires" by occupying territory for the gain of the occupying nation, whereas America establishes bases abroad to enforce the rule of international law and to secure democracy.

Gingrich's definition focuses on the necessary military buildup required to maintain America's unique role (p. 164), as well as on a spiritual basis as its underlying cause (p. 21 & 85). Gingrich previously authored a book, Real Change, expounding upon the need for a larger military; and wrote another book, Rediscovering God in America, outlining the spiritual basis of American society; this book joins those two themes together.

The GOP's interest in American exceptionalism counters Obama's rejection of the concept. When asked in 2009, Obama responded, "Sure, I believe in American exceptionalism in the same way the British believe in British exceptionalism and the Greeks believe in Greek exceptionalism." Republicans generally interpret that as meaning, "No, I don't believe in your version of American exceptionalism at all."

The GOP infer in that disagreement a self-fulfilling prophecy that America is in decline; i.e., that by denying America's role as the sole international superpower, America will eventually doom herself to not being the sole international superpower.

The Left—and Ron Paul—view American exceptionalism as just another form of imperialism. Does it matter to the people of Saudi Arabia that our bases there "protect" them from enemies in common with their dictator's enemies? Do the people of Cuba feel like the U.S. military base at Guantanamo Bay is not a land grab like any other historical invasion? No, say Chomsky and others, all imperialists justified their invasions as for the good of the world, and probably meant it as much as America does today.

Gingrich chose to publish this book at the start of the primary campaign, hence positioning American Exceptionalism as the theme for his presidential candidacy. Ron Paul warns the opposite of Gingrich's recommendation of American Exceptionalism: If America unilaterally maintains a large military abroad, America will collapse economically.

We'll see in a few decades whether Gingrich or Ron Paul were right. But I suspect we'll see in a few months that Gingrich was wrong about making Exceptionalism his campaign theme. Gingrich brilliantly implemented the Contract With America in 1984, with his hand solidly on the pulse of the electorate. But now, not only is Gingrich's hand no longer on the electorate's pulse, but Gingrich seems to not even know where to find their wrist at all. This book just screams "out of touch with the American public."

Book review written July 2011;
full excerpts available online at:
www.ontheissues.org/Nation_No_Other.htm

Book Review: End the Fed
by Rep. Ron Paul (Sept. 29, 2010)

Economics is known as "the dismal science." Rep. Ron Paul does his best in this book to explain economics entertainingly, but it's a pretty dismal book. Paul does a fine job explaining economics as well as his policy prescriptions for the economic future—but the "dismal science" topic disallows Paul's usual entertaining style. If you want to understand this economic crisis, plow through this book. But if you want an entertaining book, try Paul's other books (linked below).

The title "End the Fed" derives from a chanting crowd during the 2008 election: "The title of this book comes from a slogan that can be heard at rallies all around the country. I first heard it at the University of Michigan in October 2007. When I mentioned monetary policy, a small group chanted, 'End the Fed! End the Fed!' The whole crowd of 4,000 took up the call. Many held up burning dollar bills, as if to say to the central bank, you have done enough damage: your time is up." (p. 4)

Back to the dismal science: Some of Paul's points:

• The Fed creates money out of thin air, as opposed to basing it on gold. (pp. 2-3)

• The Fed's money monopoly depreciates the dollar (pp. 6-7)

• The Fed was founded in 1924 to end all business cycles & panics, but obviously has not (pp. 24-27)

• We should restore the gold standard (backing dollars with gold) which Nixon ended in 1971 (pp. 44-46)

Paul goes into much more technical detail on many other issues too—he really does explain how money works; how the Fed manipulates the system; and why politicians prefer to keep the system that way. If you're going to study the dismal science, and don't mind the libertarian take, this book really is the best way to learn it!

Book review written June 2011;
full excerpts available online at:
www.ontheissues.org/End_Fed.htm

Book Review: The Revolution:
A Manifesto
by Rep. Ron Paul (April 1, 2008)

This book is as close as Ron Paul's 2008 campaign gets to a campaign book. It was published in April 2008, amid Ron Paul's presidential primary campaign, and the title refers to the "Ron Paul Revolution" using the term that his supporters coined.

This book outlines Rep. Paul's general stances on the issues, both political and policy. Paul's policies are more libertarian than conservative—he opposes all government intervention, including the Iraq War. Paul clarifies here how he's often anti-Republican— bashing the GOP "Contract with America" as well as Bush's signing statements. But he is a Republican—pro-life and anti-foreign aid.

The title term "Revolution" refers to the grassroots campaign's self-described "Ron Paul Revolution." Their most substantive claim to a revolution is in how Paul's grassroots supporters—independent of the formal campaign—organized a pair of fundraising events in late 2007 that set fundraising records. The first event, on Nov. 5, a historic date known as Guy Fawkes Day, raised $4.2 million; the second event, on the anniversary of the Boston Tea Party, broke that record again.

The events were organized primarily on the internet, and while the campaign was aware of the "money bombs," the campaign itself did not organize the events. Howard Dean supporters will recognize that the techniques they pioneered in 2004 were used to great effect by Ron Paul supporters. While the Deanies in 2004 had to contend with defining FEC 527 laws and independent grassroots fundraising, the Paulistas in 2008 knew all the rules in advance. Both campaigns will presumably be used as models for future grassroots fundraising.

Paul has several more detailed books for those interested in a deeper dive into libertarian policy. The three that we've excerpted are Paul's book on foreign policy, A Foreign Policy of Freedom; on economics, Gold, Peace, and Prosperity; and on Constitutional issues, Freedom Under Siege. Those three books were written well before the presidential campaign, but have been more recently updated in some parts.

Book review written Nov. 2008;
full excerpts available online at:
www.ontheissues.org/Revolution_Manifesto.htm

Book Review: Real Change:
From the World that Fails
to the World that Works
by Speaker Newt Gingrich
(Dec. 18, 2007)

The Republican Party has failed in implementing the Revolution of 1994, and it's time to restart that Revolution again (p. 71). At least, according to Newt Gingrich, who considers himself the architect of the Revolution of 1994. This book was written in 2009, so it's unclear whether Newt considers the Tea Party to be the new Revolution (his partner in the Revolution of 1994, Rep. Dick Armey, certainly does, as outlined in his 2010 book, Give Us Liberty). It is *not* unclear, however, that Newt considers himself to be the appropriate leader for the new Revolution.

The new Revolution is needed now, says Newt, because of the losses to Obama and the Democrats: "For a number of years I kept quiet, but the recent devastation to my party is now so great that I am compelled to speak out explicitly and decisively." (p. 24). He blames partisanship on both sides of the aisle (p. 43) for the dysfunctional state of American politics: he has one chapter entitled "An Unreformed Right: Why Republicans Can't Govern Successfully"; and another entitled "An Unreformed Left: Why Democrats Can't Deliver Real Change." The solution? Go back to the non-partisanship of the Revolution of 1994.

Citizens who actually remember the Revolution of 1994, in contrast to Newt, generally consider the era to be quite partisan. Newt *does* deserve credit for "nationalizing" the Congressional election of 1994 (getting people to vote for the Contract With America as much as just for their individual Congressional race); and he *does* deserve credit for a Revolution. But he also deserves blame for the harsh partisanship that characterized the House of Representatives in the 1990s, culminating in Bill Clinton's impeachment, arguably the most partisan act in American history. Citizens might also contrast Newt's view with the fact that he resigned from the House speakership in the wake of a government shutdown—also an intensely partisan act.

Nevertheless, Newt is back, and he is running for President. This book is just the first salvo in his battle for the GOP nomination. He has prepared appropriately: he formed several political organizations in the past decade to bolster his credentials on key issues (each of which gets a plug for its website, p. xxi):

- The Center for Health Transformation (www. HealthTransformation.net)

- American Solutions for Winning the Future (www. AmericanSolutions.com)

- Renewing American Leadership (ReAL, www.RenewingAmericanLeadership.com)

If Newt does enter the Republican primary, he is sure to be great entertainment. While Newt is renowned for his slightly non-mainstream academic analysis, listeners accept it as mainstream because he delivers it with such certitude (almost always in this book, the passive voice is used, to illustrate how it's obvious that most voters are in agreement). His analysis is data-driven and historical (he's a history professor, after all), although some might call that "wonkish," a sure-fire losing attitude since Dukakis' days. Newt would call his attitude "futuristic," since his hero is still Alvin Toffler, author of "Future Shock" and "The Third Wave" (p. 65).

Whether wonkish or futuristic, Newt will be non-mainstream and hence entertaining. For example, he proposes (in the passive voice) that the US should invade Pakistan: "Afghanistan would have been dealt with in a regional context that would have included the Waziristan section of Pakistan." (p. 305). And maybe invade Syria and others too (also in the passive voice): "There would have been no free passage through Damascus for foreign terrorists to come kill Americans," but that wouldn't actually require invasions because the dictators might yield once they saw "the fury of the American people mobilized to action."

In summary, Newt positions himself as the conservative choice: more hawkish than the GOP hawks; more anti-Obama than the rest of the GOP; and more "change" than Obama ever offered. Newt will have a lot of trouble with the conservatives accepting his three divorces; he'll have even more trouble with the general electorate accepting his conversion to non-partisanship; and he'll have the most trouble of all with voters who remember him as the past generation instead of the future. But he'll be a heck of a lot of fun!

Book review written April 2011;
full excerpts available online at:
www.ontheissues.org/Real_Change.htm

Book Review:
Rediscovering God in America:
Reflections on the Role of
Faith in Our Nation's History and Future
by Speaker Newt Gingrich
(Oct. 10, 2006)

Newt Gingrich in this book expresses strongly how important God has been to American history. The structure of this book is a "tour" of Washington DC, pointing out all of the references to God built into our public monuments and buildings, as well as in their design and history. The details of that aspect of the book are mostly omitted here because OnTheIssues doesn't have categories for history nor architecture.

But there is a political purpose too, and those comprise our excerpts. In particular, Gingrich applies the historical importance of God in America to examine numerous current public policy issues, from the Pledge of Allegiance to school prayer. Gingrich reserves particular venom for the US Supreme Court and other courts who rule in favor of omitting God from public displays—claiming that they are usurping power intended for the legislature, and also ignoring the importance of God in centuries of American history.

This book is similar in conclusions to Mike Huckabee's Character Makes a Difference. Gov. Huckabee, however, comes from a pastoral perspective, arguing on religious and moral grounds instead of Gingrich's historical grounds. Gingrich's argument is certainly more effective when attempting to persuade non-Christians or secularists.

This book is similar in conclusions to Mike Huckabee's Character Makes a Difference. Gov. Huckabee, however, comes from a pastoral perspective, arguing on religious and moral grounds instead of Gingrich's historical grounds. Gingrich's argument is certainly more effective when attempting to persuade non-Christians or secularists.

Book review written May 2007;
full excerpts available online at:
www.ontheissues.org/Rediscovering_God.htm

Paul vs. Gingrich on VoteMatch

VoteMatch is our 20-question quiz which summarizes the candidate's views on the controversial issues of the day.

VoteMatch Social Issues

	Ron Paul	Newt Gingrich
Abortion is a woman's right	opposes	strongly opposes
Require companies to hire more women & minorities	strongly opposes	strongly opposes
Same-sex domestic partnership benefits	favors	opposes
Teacher-led prayer in public schools	favors	strongly favors
Parents choose schools via vouchers	favors	strongly favors

VoteMatch Domestic Issues

	Ron Paul	Newt Gingrich
More federal funding for health coverage	opposes	strongly opposes
Death Penalty	strongly opposes	strongly favors
Mandatory Three Strikes sentencing laws	opposes	favors
Absolute right to gun ownership	favors	favors
Drug use is immoral: enforce laws against it	strongly opposes	strongly favors

VoteMatch Economic Issues

	Ron Paul	Newt Gingrich
Privatize Social Security	strongly favors	strongly favors
Make taxes more progressive	strongly opposes	opposes
Stricter limits on political campaign funds	opposes	strongly opposes
Allow churches to provide welfare services	favors	favors
Replace coal & oil with alternatives	strongly opposes	strongly opposes

VoteMatch International Issues

	Ron Paul	Newt Gingrich
Illegal immigrants earn citizenship	strongly opposes	neutral
Support & expand free trade	opposes	favors
The Patriot Act harms civil liberties	strongly favors	strongly opposes
Expand the armed forces	opposes	strongly favors
US out of Iraq & Afghanistan	strongly favors	favors

In our online quiz, you fill in your answers for these 20 questions, and we match you against all the candidates. Please see:

http://quiz.ontheissues.org/

Afterword

We hope that this book encourages you, as voters, to make your decisions based on the issues. We recognize the reality of American politics: voters make their decisions based primarily on whether they like the candidates. Accordingly, our goal is to get voters to compare their issue preferences in comparison to candidate issue stances when considering which candidates to like.

We intentionally omitted from this book any biographical background on Rep. Paul and Speaker Gingrich. Details of their birthplaces and religious affiliations—and minutiae of every other personal detail—are readily available in the mainstream media. Their issue stances are more challenging for voters to find.

Why does the mainstream media fail at this important function? Because they are "news" organizations which are poorly suited to covering political campaigns. "News" implies reporting on what is "new": Gingrich's stance on the War on Drugs has not changed since 1998, and Paul's stance on the Gold standard has not changed since 1981, so there's nothing in the news about those issues. But if you are impassioned about the Drug War, or if you vote based on Fed policy, then you cannot rely on the news media for those non-newsworthy issues. And that's where we come in.

This book represents an archive of where these two candidates stand on the key issues of our time. We don't consider whether candidates' issue stances are new—just what they say on each issue. That often requires a lot of digging on our part—we have a team of researchers to do that, but we invite you to volunteer any issue stances that we don't cover.

Our online website www.ontheissues.org covers many more issues than can fit in any book: many more stances from Romney and Perry, as well as all of the other 2012 candidates, Governors, Senators, and House members. We score each candidate on a 20-question quiz called "VoteMatch." A representation of the VoteMatch quiz results for the presidential contenders appears on the back cover of this book. The mainstream media interpret candidates using a one-dimensional "right-left" analysis. That simplistic analysis comes to nonsensical conclusions like calling Ron Paul "extreme right-wing" even though he opposes the Iraq War; opposes the PATRIOT Act; supports drug legalization; and supports same-sex domestic partnership benefits.

We find our two-dimensional analysis to be more accurate in differentiating candidates than that traditional one-dimensional analysis. We don't claim that our method is perfect—just superior to the simplistic mainstream media. VoteMatch uses a Social Issues dimension plus an Economic Issues dimension; we interpret candidates based on whether they believe in government involvement in either or both of those dimensions. Using the two-dimensional analysis differentiates five classes of political beliefs:

1. *Libertarian:*
   No government involvement in social issues
   No government involvement in economic issues

2. *Conservative:*
   Government involvement in social issues
   No government involvement in economic issues

3. *Liberal:*
   No government involvement in social issues
   Government involvement in economic issues

4. *Populist:*
   Government involvement in social issues
   Government involvement in economic issues

5. *Centrist:*
   Some government involvement in social issues
   Some government involvement in economic issues

Most importantly, you can answer the same 20 questions and see *your* political label and how the candidates match up with *you*. We invite you to try the VoteMatch quiz at:

http://quiz.ontheissues.org

Other Books in This Series

About the Author

Jesse Gordon has been the editor-in-chief of OnTheIssues.org since its formation in 1999. His passion revolves around providing issue-based coverage on political races, to combat the mainstream media's growing lack of such coverage.

Mr. Gordon holds a Master's degree in Public Policy from Harvard University's Kennedy School of Government. He and the website OnTheIssues.org are based in Cambridge, Massachusetts. He resides with his fiancée, Kathleen; his son Julien; Kathleen's son Derek; their cat Chanel; and six fish with whom Chanel is obsessed.

Mr. Gordon replies to email personally, at jesse@ontheissues. org—whether to suggest improvements to the website or to order one of the other books above.

www.ingramcontent.com/pod-product-compliance
Lightning Source LLC
Chambersburg PA
CBHW061303280526
45784CB00002B/879